Gifted and Talented in the Early Years

Books

Gifted and Talented in the Early Years

Practical Activities for Children aged 3 to 5

Margaret Sutherland

Paul Chapman Publishing
London · Thousand Oaks · New Delhi

Paul Chapman Publishing
A SAGE Publications Company
1 Oliver's Yard
55 City Road
London EC1Y 1SP

SAGE Publications Inc
2455 Teller Road
Thousand Oaks, California 91320

SAGE Publications India Pvt Ltd
B-42 Panchsheel Enclave
Post Box 4109
New Delhi 110 017

Library of Congress Control Number: 2005900432

A catalogue record for this book is available from the British Library

ISBN 1-4129-0367-X
ISBN 1-4129-0368-8 (pbk)

Typeset by Pantek Arts Ltd, Maidstone, Kent
Printed in Great Britain by Cromwell Press Ltd, Wiltshire

Contents

About the author

Margaret Sutherland is a lecturer in additional support needs at the University of Glasgow. She has 23 years' teaching experience in mainstream primary schools, behaviour support and latterly in higher education. She has written articles in the field of gifted and talented education. She speaks regularly at conferences and leads courses, workshops and seminars across the country.

Acknowledgements

My thanks go to Kirsteen who, as an inspirational five-year-old pupil in my class, set me off in the direction of gifted and talented education.

Thanks, too, go to the staff and children of Killermont Primary School and Nursery, Bearsden and Lenzie Primary School and Nursery, Lenzie. In particular I would like to thank Shona Mathieson, Susan May, Harji Kaur and Mairi Gillies for allowing me to visit their early years settings and for offering helpful and supportive comments at each stage of writing.

Advice and support were gratefully received from my colleagues and friends, Chris Smith and Rae Galbraith and from Jude Bowen and Charlotte Saunders at SAGE Publications.

Finally my thanks go to Andrew and Briagh for 'putting up with me' during the writing process.

Dedication

For all children I have worked with – for those I discovered who were gifted and talented and for the ones I missed because I didn't look in the right place or offer the right opportunities and challenges.

Preface

The importance of early education cannot be underestimated. A love of learning and a sense of excitement, purpose and creativity formed in the early years can go on to have lasting impact on the lives of young people. Opportunities offered in the early years can develop into lifelong passions, giving our world a diversity and richness that can only enhance and augment the lives of all. As someone working with young children you are in ideal situation to offer these opportunities. It is a very privileged position to be in and one we need to take seriously if we are to help young children develop in a way that celebrates and cultivates their full range of abilities and aptitudes.

If you're reading this book then it is likely that you have in your care a child who is demonstrating abilities beyond what might be expected for their age. These children, sometimes referred to as 'tall poppies', will be doing things in your early years setting that often leave you standing in amazement – such as the three-year-old child who goes into the story corner and reads a book for themselves. There is no doubt that young children are often capable of more than we think. National initiatives in the UK (Early Intervention, Scotland; Foundation Stage, England and Wales) have helped to raise expectations among educators. Perhaps less well documented are the group of children who often receive the label 'gifted and talented'. It is the educational experiences of these children that this book will explore.

International (UN, 1992; UN, 1989) and national (SOEID, 1994; SEED, 2003; DfES, 1998, 2001) initiatives have seen an ever-increasing move towards inclusive education. There is much debate as to what this term means and there are a plethora of books on the market that consider just this issue. For the purposes of this book, 'inclusive education' is taken to mean children learning together: learning from each other, from adults around them and from their communities and families. The focus of this book will be to explore how we can meet the needs of the so-called 'tall poppies' mentioned above within an inclusive education framework.

The first chapter of this book sets out to explore the nature of intelligence. It considers the labels we use to describe gifted and talented children and looks at how the adult's beliefs about intelligence will impact on what they do, say and look for in the early years setting. It challenges educators to think about the nature of intelligence.

Chapter 2 investigates the tricky area of identification. It suggests practical ways of identifying young gifted and talented learners – interview questions, observation sheets and tracking sheets are suggested as ways of building up an 'holistic picture' of a child and their abilities. Once this information has been gathered, the chapter considers how you link that information to national documentation in order to develop challenging learning experiences.

Chapter 3 considers four curriculum areas – physical movement/motor development, music, language and mathematics – and offers some suggestions as to what may be advanced responses to common early years activities and resources in these areas.

The next four chapters, Chapters 4–7, consider each individual curricular area and contain ideas for challenging activities. The activity sheets can be used as they appear or can be adapted and developed to suit individual settings. These chapters may be 'dipped in and out of' as a particular need in a particular curricular area arises.

The final chapter pulls together the thoughts and ideas from throughout the book. It highlights the need to challenge our gifted and talented children and to ensure that we offer challenging learning opportunities for all.

You will see three icons appearing throughout the book:

 This icon indicates that there are some key points that early educators should bear in mind when working with young gifted and talented learners.

This icon suggests some points for good practice.

This icon means you can photocopy the pages.

It should be noted that the four countries that make up the United Kingdom have adopted slightly different terminology:

Scotland: more able pupils

Northern Ireland: gifted children

Wales: more able and talented pupils

England: gifted and talented

Chapter 1

Intelligence – what is it?

Some key points about the education of gifted and talented learners will be made in this chapter.

- Adopting an inclusive approach to learning is helpful to young gifted and talented learners.

- Current learning theory offers an opportunity to ensure all abilities are being challenged and celebrated.

- Culture plays a part in the learning process.

- Labels for gifted and talented learners, while useful, can also be a hindrance. We need to focus on what the labels mean and try to come to some shared understandings about the terms used.

- Intelligence is difficult to define. It is our beliefs about intelligence that will influence our view of children in the early years setting and impact on individuals' self-beliefs.

WHO ARE THE GIFTED AND TALENTED IN YOUR EARLY YEARS SETTING?

I wonder what picture you have in your mind of a child who is gifted and talented? Often we conjure up images of a round-faced kid with freckles and glasses. He/she always answers questions correctly and is often to be found on his/her own, usually doing science experiments. He/she is sometimes known as 'the little professor'. Or perhaps it is the virtuoso violin player who happens to be four years old. He/she spends hours practising almost to the exclusion of everything else; he/she is quietly spoken and is good at mathematics as well. This kind of stereotyping, while common, is not helpful, particularly if we're considering the education of young gifted and talented children within an inclusive education framework. For many, these narrow views of who the gifted and talented are will go on to shape and influence what they do with young children in their care.

The early years setting is the ideal place to discuss the education of gifted and talented children within an inclusive education framework. Young children are, more often than not, very accepting of others who are in some way 'different'. While their honesty can be refreshing, although sometimes embarrassing for adults, by and large young children accept others for who they are and will play happily alongside each other, often seeming to be oblivious to the differences that exist. However, for adults, this acceptance does not always come quite so easily. When we see a child doing something that is unusual in some way we often seek to identify what it is that is different and then we go about finding a label to explain this difference. We may even try to 'fix' the difference, just so they're 'normal'.

INCLUSION IN THE EARLY YEARS SETTING

Early years settings, by their very nature, are often considered to be inclusive in the care and education of young children. The structure and practice within early years settings would seem to allow for the adoption of an inclusive approach to learning. For one thing, a play-centred curriculum allows for a child-centred approach: children drive the learning process. This is not to say that there is no structure and that goals are not set, it's just that learning and development are seen as important and not simply targets and results. Traditionally in the UK education systems we have excluded 'children that don't fit' – those with physical impairment, behaviour difficulties, learning difficulties and yes … even the gifted and talented. However, often in the early years setting these children are educated alongside one another and it is only on entry to formal school that division occurs.

A danger when early years settings start to identify gifted and talented learners is that they lose what makes the early years setting experience unique and child-centred and instead start to adopt the formal approaches offered in schools. That young gifted and talented learners need to be challenged is not debatable; how we do this perhaps requires further discussion. For the purposes of this book, inclusive education is taken to mean children learning together: learning from each other, from adults around them and from their communities and families. In this way, it is argued, gifted and talented learners can be:

- challenged appropriately

- seen as valuable members of the learning community

- have their gifts and talents recognised and celebrated

within an inclusive setting.

So what do we know about learning that will help us to do this?

LEARNING IN THE EARLY YEARS SETTING

Much has been written about learning and how we learn. Advances in science and medicine, for example, mean we now know much more than we did in the past about how our brain functions and the impact that this has on learning. However, this knowledge has not always changed what we do as educators.

A number of theories have developed about learning. Any theory reflects a 'moment' in time. Theories come and go and collapse in on themselves when society changes. We learn new things that suggest the theory needs to change, adapt or be modified. This can give the impression that we are going round in circles.

However, there are some key things we know about learning that are important and will maximise learning for all learners:

- Learning is a social activity.

- Children learn best from collaborative activities.

- Experiences gained outside of early years setting should be linked to the learning taking place in the early years setting.

- Learning in early years settings should be contextualised and not divorced from real-world experiences.

Taking these points into account, there are a number of core principles that underpin good learning experiences for all children. Bearing in mind this includes those who are gifted and talented, some principles might be:

- All children have a right to an education that is appropriately challenging and takes account of individual needs.

- Each person has a unique profile across a wide range of abilities that should be recognised, enhanced and valued equally.

- Recognition of an individual's ability profile is only possible in partnership with parents and other significant individuals in that person's life.

- Appropriate challenge must be provided at all points on an individual's ability profile.

- The key to recognition of an individual's abilities lies with the provision of appropriately challenging opportunities.

● Errors are critical to the learning process thus appropriately challenging opportunities may require challenges that take the individual to the point of failure. This is only possible, however, within an ethos where it is safe to fail.

● An inclusive education system is the most supportive framework for offering opportunities to prevent underachievement and provide appropriate challenge across the ability range.

(Scottish Network for Able Pupils, 2004)

These principles form the framework for learning discussed in subsequent chapters and if adopted would offer a framework for addressing the needs of gifted and talented learners.

LEARNING AND CULTURE

An educational theorist called Jerome Bruner argues that culture shapes the mind and is shaped by the mind and that this gives us the mechanism by which we can make sense of the world and our place within it. He talks about the 'culture of childhood' (Bruner, 1996). Any thinking in which we engage is therefore rooted in our culture.

The *Collins Concise English Dictionary* defines *culture* as

> *the total of the inherited ideas, beliefs, values and knowledge, which constitute the shared basis of social action.* (Collins, 1988)

The communities that you and your children come from will have definite cultures. Often communities can be melting pots of cultural experiences and exchanges but it is likely that out of this will come a dominant culture and it is this which will influence you, the children and their families. We are all products of our different cultures. This will impact on your thinking and understanding of learning.

As well as a national and local or community culture, there will be an early years setting culture. This is influenced and shaped by management. There will be a culture within your room that has been created and shaped by your experiences and the experiences of those in the room. It may change from year to year as you work with different year groups. It will undoubtedly influence how you approach tasks and interact with the children and each other.

If we want to support young children in their learning, we need to have an understanding of the significant influences on their lives. What they believe and are influenced by may well affect how they approach life in an early years setting. What you believe and are influenced by will affect your expectations and how you approach the early years setting. Arriving at some shared understanding of this may help us to support the children's learning.

This idea of culture is important when we start to think about young children who are gifted and talented. Different cultural perspectives, both yours and those of the children and their families, will influence learning in your early years setting. Some children will come from homes where learning and education are revered; others will come from homes where education is secondary to dealing with life issues.

Your ideas about learning and ability will be based on:

- your own experiences

- the culture from which you come

- the culture in which you work.

- We need to be aware of the dominant culture.

- We need to be aware of the impact culture has on learning.

- We need to consider what kind of culture we have developed in our early years setting.

LABELS IN AN EARLY YEARS SETTING

We like the world to make sense and to help us we often label things. So the young child who learns the word 'bath' refers to all water as 'bath'. This gives us a sense of order and comfort. As adults we still seek to label things in order to categorise and for ease of explanation. In the case of young gifted and talented children, there are a plethora of labels used to describe them. Indeed, these labels are often attributed to all children who show particular aptitude.

Here are just some of the more common words and phrases used in the UK:

- Smart
- Bright
- Precocious
- Clever
- Switched on
- Bright as a button
- Smart cookie

- Bright spark
- Clever clogs
- High achiever
- More able
- Special aptitude
- Gifted
- Talented

Each one of these words or phrases brings with it 'baggage' – particular connotations and meanings. How adults view children's abilities will often depend on the adult's view of intelligence; this in turn will influence their choice of description and indeed will influence whether the adult thinks that the ability being demonstrated is worthwhile and worthy of a label in the first place. Let's unpack these labels a little and see what lies behind them.

Traditionally in the UK we have tended to equate intelligence with mathematical and linguistic aptitude. Abilities that fall outside these domains are often not recognised. Many of the labels listed above are used to describe children who have shown aptitude in mathematics and language. So you will hear the four-year-old who can read being described as 'a real bright spark'. Likewise children who have ability in mathematics will often be described as 'gifted' or 'a real smart cookie'. Because words and phrases mean different things to different people, we can end up with staff in an early years setting all using the same word or words but actually talking about different things. The danger is not in the fact that we all use different words to describe abilities and children, it is that we assign different value and meaning to different words. Similarly, if all staff in the early years setting hold a very narrow view of what it is to be intelligent, then abilities that lie outside the narrow definition are unlikely to be recognised or challenged.

While labels can sometimes be helpful they can also cause problems. For example:

- we don't all use the same words to describe the same abilities

- they can set up misleading expectations – for children, parents and staff

- people look no further than the label

- they lead to a child only being challenged in what they are already good at

- they might be limiting and disguise the child's other abilities.

Therefore it might be more beneficial to focus on what lies behind these labels. If we can start to come to some kind of shared understanding as to what we think being gifted and talented might mean, then we can start to think about what we value and how we can challenge the abilities that the children in our care demonstrate. In other words, let's not agonise over what label we assign but instead let's engage in discussion about what the words actually mean to us.

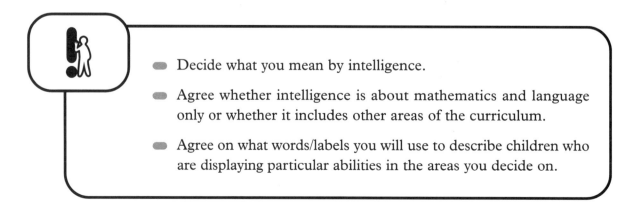

- Decide what you mean by intelligence.

- Agree whether intelligence is about mathematics and language only or whether it includes other areas of the curriculum.

- Agree on what words/labels you will use to describe children who are displaying particular abilities in the areas you decide on.

WHAT IS INTELLIGENCE?

Just what does it mean to be intelligent? For years we have tried to describe what being intelligent means but perhaps there is no one definition of intelligence. Intelligence is often measured by standardised tests that the child has taken, from which their IQ is established. To suggest that a certain percentage of children are 'intelligent' by reference to a single test score is neither helpful to the identification procedure nor to selecting the most effective form of provision (Koshy and Casey, 1997). The test may have been standardised on a population that was vastly different from the one to which the child being tested belongs. Not only is the population different, but also cultural differences may be significant to the outcome of the test. Neither do such tests take account of creativity or divergent thinking – abilities which a gifted and talented child will often demonstrate. David George (1997) suggests that while an IQ test may allow the identification of some children with certain abilities, it may be more to do with the fact that these children:

> *perform well in academic subjects … are persistent, respond well to instruction, have good study skills … process information quickly, have better memories, have greater accuracy and are good at abstract thinking.*   (George, 1997, p. 37)

In other words, they're good at passing tests!

This still leaves us with our original question – what does it mean to be intelligent? The work of Howard Gardner (1983) in the USA encouraged us to think differently about intelligence. He suggested that intelligence is not just about maths and language but included a much wider range of abilities. He also argued we all have all of them to a greater or lesser degree and they are not hierarchical. Gardner's list includes:

- linguistic intelligence (Word smart)
- mathematical intelligence (Logic smart)
- interpersonal intelligence (People smart)
- naturalist intelligence (Nature smart)
- visual-spatial intelligence (Picture smart)
- musical intelligence (Music smart)
- bodily kinaesthetic intelligence (Body smart)
- intrapersonal intelligence (Self smart)
- existential intelligence (Wonder smart).

What would young children be doing if they were demonstrating abilities in these areas? Table 1.1 gives some examples.

Table 1.1 **Abilities associated with different intelligences**

Intelligence	Evidence	Famous people
Linguistic (word smart)	• Tells stories and jokes • Good memory for names, dates, etc. • Enjoys word games • Likes tongue twisters • Has a good vocabulary • Communicates well	• Shakespeare • Hemmingway • J.K. Rowling • Agatha Christie • Elizabeth Barrett Browning
Logical/mathematical (number smart)	• Plays chess and strategy games • Understands cause and effect • Asks questions about how things work • Can do arithmetic in their heads quickly	• Archimedes • Sir Isaac Newton • Einstein
Interpersonal (people smart)	• Enjoys being with peers • A natural leader • Offers advice to friends • Has close friends • Others want to be their friend	• Oprah Winfrey • Abraham Lincoln • Gandhi • Martin Luther King
Naturalist (nature smart)	• Enjoys learning about animals or nature • An interest in biology, zoology, geology, astronomy • Aware of the environment • Categorises easily • Likes beauty and the outside world	• Galileo • Jacques Cousteau • Dian Fossey
Visual/Spatial (picture smart)	• Reads maps, charts and diagrams easily • Enjoys puzzles, jigsaws, I spy • Builds 3-dimensional constructions • Draws in advance of age • Understands pictures more than words	• Michelangelo • Picasso • Steven Spielberg • Monet
Musical (music smart)	• Knows when music is 'off key' • Remembers the tune to a song • Sings well • Can keep the rhythm • Imitates others easily • Plays an instrument	• Mozart • Beethoven • Scott Joplin • John Lennon

Table 1.1   continued...

Intelligence	Evidence	Famous people
Bodily kinaesthetic (body smart)	<ul><li>Good at sports</li><li>Can mimic gestures</li><li>Good fine-motor skills</li><li>Likes plasticine, clay and hands on art activities</li><li>Has difficulty sitting still</li><li>Very active</li></ul>	<ul><li>Tiger Woods</li><li>Marcel Marceau</li><li>David Beckham</li><li>Wayne Rooney</li></ul>
Intrapersonal (self smart)	<ul><li>Independent</li><li>Plays well alone</li><li>Aware of strengths/weakness</li><li>Can express how they are feeling</li><li>Learns from mistakes</li></ul>	<ul><li>Joan of Arc</li><li>Sir Edmund Hillary</li><li>Neil Armstrong</li><li>Columbus</li></ul>
Existential (wonder smart)	<ul><li>Asks big questions about life/death</li><li>Asks questions about other planets</li><li>Appears to be fully aware of the cosmos</li><li>Asks life's larger questions</li></ul>	<ul><li>Aristotle</li><li>Confucius</li><li>Einstein</li><li>Plato</li><li>Socrates</li></ul>

This wider approach to intelligence links well with existing work in the early years setting and allows for an holistic or whole-person approach to development and the recognition of abilities. However, in spite of this wider approach it is often children who display abilities in mathematics (logic smart) and language (word smart) that are identified.

An American psychologist called Carol Dweck (1999) has considered theories of intelligence. She has spilt these into two broad categories – entity theory of intelligence and incremental theory of intelligence.

Holding an **entity view of intelligence** will mean believing a person possesses a specific amount of intelligence and nothing you or they can do will change that amount. In other words:

- it's fixed

- you've only got so much of it

- there's not much you can do about how much you've got

- there's nothing you can do as the educator to increase the amount they've got.

If you hold this belief you are likely to say the following things:

Well, you can't make a silk purse out of a sow's ear

She's tried hard; she just hasn't got what it takes

You can try as hard as you like, but if the child hasn't got it in them, there's nothing you can do

Holding an **incremental view of intelligence** will mean believing that intelligence is not an 'entity' that resides within a person but is something that can be developed through learning. In other words:

- it can change

- you can become more intelligent

- the more you learn, the more you can learn

- the educator can work with the person so they become more intelligent.

If you hold this belief you are likely to say the following things:

The harder you work the more intelligent you'll become

It's all right to make mistakes, that's how we learn

We can work on this problem together and we'll sort it out

Dweck uses these two categories – entity and incremental – to explain people's understanding of, and beliefs about, intelligence. It is these beliefs about intelligence that will influence our expectations of children and our approaches to working with children.

These two very different beliefs will result in very different behaviours within individuals. For example, Dweck suggests the following:

Learning is fixed (entity)	Learning can change (incremental)
worry about how much fixed intelligence they have	believe everyone with effort and guidance can incraese their intellectual abilities
need to look and feel like they have enough 'intelligence'	need to learn
need to look smart and need to out-perform others	sacrifice opportunities to look smart in favour of opportunities to learn something new
need easy successes	thrive on challenge

(Dweck, 1999, p. 3)

These beliefs about intelligence are closely linked to what Dweck calls 'goal achievement' (Dweck, 1999). By this she means that if you hold a fixed view of intelligence then it will be performance goals that will be important to you because you need to show just how clever and smart you are. In contrast, if you possess an incremental view of intelligence then you will be concerned with becoming smarter and so learning goals will be more important to you.

Dweck found out that your belief about intelligence greatly influences how you approach tasks. Those who believed intelligence was fixed opted for easier tasks that would make them look smart and those who thought it could change sought out interesting, challenging tasks that would forward their learning.

YOUNG CHILDREN'S IDEAS ABOUT INTELLIGENCE

Often children arrive in the early years setting with definite views about themselves and their abilities. How often have you heard the statement 'I can't do difficult jigsaws, only easy ones'? There could be a number of reasons for this type of response.

At one time people believed that young children didn't really understand the concept of intelligence. When a young child 'failed' at a task it was believed that this failure didn't automatically lead to pessimistic feelings about themselves and their abilities, as it seemed to in older children. However, the work of Dweck and others challenged this idea.

Dweck suggests that young children are not so much interested in intelligence; this she argues develops as the child becomes older. Rather, children are concerned with ideas about 'goodness' and 'badness'. This can be seen in the early years setting and in life generally as young children explore and often challenge the rules and possibilities that are set before them. Interaction with and reaction from family members, peers and adults in the early years setting all help the young child to begin to build up a picture of themselves. Perhaps that's where the statement about the jigsaws came from. Dweck argues that vulnerable young children 'feel they are bad when they encounter failure or criticism. And – just like older children with intelligence – they think that badness is a stable trait' (Dweck, 1999, p. 97). If young children grow up believing that mistakes and failure are bad and it therefore makes them feel bad, then it is likely that they will spend much of their time avoiding making mistakes. This is not helpful if we accept that mistakes are a vital part of the learning process. There is also evidence to suggest that if they accept that this 'badness' or 'failure' is innate, in other words fixed, then they believe there's nothing they can do about it. When later these ideas of 'goodness' and 'badness' or 'failure' and 'success' are transported into school and academic life it is perhaps hardly surprising that we find children who are desperate to show you how clever or smart they are. They need you to know 'I'm not stupid'. From an early age learners start to evaluate their own abilities and so build up a personal theory relating to intelligence. Information that helps them to do this comes from three sources:

- through comparison with others

- through feedback from significant others

- through interactions within their own particular contexts.

(McLean, 2003)

The good news is that we can influence young children's views of themselves so they become interested in learning, but how we influence children's views will depend on our own beliefs about intelligence.

To influence children's views about themselves in a positive way, educators need to:

- believe that intelligence is not fixed

- acknowledge that genetics plays a part but not 'write children off' because of who their parents are

- encourage young children to make mistakes and learn from them

- praise the amount of effort a child puts into an activity.

FIXED OR CHANGEABLE? WHAT DOES THIS MEAN FOR THE EARLY YEARS SETTING?

So what does all this mean for our gifted and talented learners, and us as adults, working in the early years setting? Two things are important here in relation to your work in the early years setting:

1. Your view of intelligence will influence how you view children in the early years setting.

2. You can influence children's views about intelligence and their ideas about their own intelligence.

Let's think for a minute about how the two different theoretical approaches/views might manifest themselves in everyday life in the early years setting.

A person with a fixed view of intelligence is likely to say the following:

> Robin is a very bright boy. He's very good at numbers. He always gets all the number activities right first time. He can be a bit of a show-off actually. Of course his dad is a joiner, he's very good at numbers, and his big sister was good too, it runs in the family.

A person who thinks intelligence can change is likely to comment:

> Robin loves numbers, works very hard at number activities and works out number puzzles quickly. He needs a challenge, as often the number activities are simple for him. His big sister liked numbers too and his dad's a joiner, perhaps they help him at home.

These two slightly different approaches are underpinned by divergent philosophies and if Robin is the recipient of one approach over the other it is likely to result in Robin approaching numbers in a particular way.

In our first scenario the adult believes this ability in number is innate and inherited. There is an assumption that Robin is naturally good with numbers and that in fact he's so good he shows off about it. Robin will learn from this that:

- your abilities are not always appreciated and are perhaps something you should keep quiet about

- he should always find number activities easy.

Over time staff may assume that Robin will be good at number activities. They may:

- try to catch him out with something in order to show him he 'doesn't know it all', or

- be pleased when he finds a particular number task difficult and challenging.

In the second scenario the staff member believes that Robin puts considerable effort into his number tasks and this effort may occur in the early years setting or at home with siblings. Either way, the staff member does not suggest that this ability in number just happens. They also acknowledge that Robin requires challenge, suggesting that number tasks should not always come easily. Robin will learn that effort is expected and that it is this effort that helps him to succeed at numbers.

Early years practitioners will:

- offer support and strategies when tasks are difficult
- encourage him to adopt new number strategies and work alongside others.

That Robin undoubtedly has a propensity towards numbers is not being denied here, but the crucial difference between this view and the view outlined previously is that this ability is developing because of support, challenging activities and effort on Robin's part and not simply because he has some predisposition to mathematics.

How we react to children will also be influenced by our underlying beliefs and these may be inadvertently transferred to the child. While a response such as 'well done, you've got these all right. You're really clever' may seem to be supportive, there is evidence to suggest that over time when it is the child we praise, suggesting that there is some innate, inherent ability, it will lead the child to assume he or she is 'clever'. When they meet difficulty and failure they will assume they can't do the task because they are not clever enough. After all, they have always been clever in the past – hasn't the early years setting supervisor always told them that? Comments such as 'you've tried really hard there. Well done,' on the other hand, will mean that when meeting with failure it is not their intelligence or ability that is being called into question but perhaps it is just a different way of approaching the task that is required. After all, they have always tried really hard in the past – hasn't the early years setting supervisor always told them that?

These two simple illustrations begin to demonstrate how over time our beliefs and reactions will impact on a child and will contribute towards their view of themselves either as individuals who can learn more and go on learning or as individuals who have learned as much as they are capable of learning.

The early years setting that considers intelligence to be multifaceted and something that can be developed will promote the identification of gifted and talented children in a broader and more inclusive way.

SUMMING UP

Some key points about the education of gifted and talented learners have been made in this chapter.

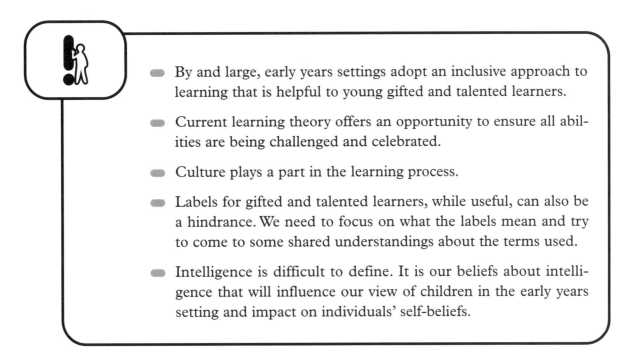

- By and large, early years settings adopt an inclusive approach to learning that is helpful to young gifted and talented learners.

- Current learning theory offers an opportunity to ensure all abilities are being challenged and celebrated.

- Culture plays a part in the learning process.

- Labels for gifted and talented learners, while useful, can also be a hindrance. We need to focus on what the labels mean and try to come to some shared understandings about the terms used.

- Intelligence is difficult to define. It is our beliefs about intelligence that will influence our view of children in the early years setting and impact on individuals' self-beliefs.

Chapter 2

Identification

Some key points about the identification of gifted and talented learners will be made in this chapter.

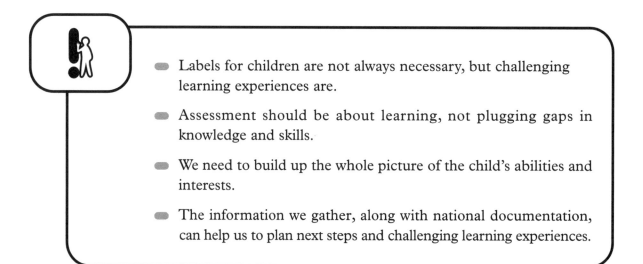

- Labels for children are not always necessary, but challenging learning experiences are.

- Assessment should be about learning, not plugging gaps in knowledge and skills.

- We need to build up the whole picture of the child's abilities and interests.

- The information we gather, along with national documentation, can help us to plan next steps and challenging learning experiences.

TO LABEL OR NOT TO LABEL?

People working in early years settings must avoid falling into the trap of thinking that they know who the gifted and talented are simply because they possess particular dispositions. For example, children are often identified as being gifted and talented if they are:

- articulate

- confident

- read well and early

- born during September to December

- mature

- vivacious

- charismatic

or have

- 'bright' elder siblings

- a good general knowledge

- good fine and gross motor skills.

Contrast this with children who:

- are quiet and withdrawn

- struggle with words

- have poor fine and gross motor skills

- have a summer birthday

- are dishevelled

- are unappealing

- have English as a second language.

These children are less likely to be immediately considered to be gifted and talented. Discovery of abilities, therefore, must be the focus of the early years setting. Offering a wide and varied range of opportunities to all will allow young children to explore and uncover the abilities they possess. The early years setting would do well to concentrate on maximising opportunities for learning. It is this that will allow gifted and talented learners to blossom and be identified, rather than some predetermined set of assumptions.

However, if, as was suggested in Chapter 1, you've arrived at a working definition of what it means to be gifted and talented, you will now be keen to find out how many of the children you work with might have gifts and/or talents that need to be challenged and developed. So what do we do? The easy answer is identify them. However, the identification of gifted and talented children is a thorny subject. If it were as simple as ticking boxes on a checklist we wouldn't need chapters on identification. Since we are talking about human beings and attributes, it follows that neat checklists will only go some way to helping us identify children and their abilities. But perhaps there is an even more fundamental question we need to be asking ourselves – if, as I have suggested previously, labelling can be dangerous as well as helpful, then should we be seeking to identify children in the early years setting as gifted and talented at all?

There is an anxiety on the part of educators and parents that labelling a child as gifted and talented at an early age may result in the following:

- being isolated from their peers (Gross, 1993)

- once labelled, 'hot-housing' may occur during which time young children may 'switch off' their special talent or ability (Mares, 1991)

- over the years other children may 'catch up' with the 'gifted and talented' children and so while still 'very good', they no longer merit the label 'gifted and talented'.

The effect of all this on children may be detrimental to learning in the long term. Parents too may feel 'under pressure' or confused. While care must be taken to avoid such scenarios, it should not be at the expense of providing appropriate and challenging activities for young children. Concern can lead to inactivity. I would suggest that we should not worry too much about the label but instead should gather information about the child that allows us to offer appropriate challenging learning experiences. In other words, let's improve assessment, which will allow us to identify children.

ASSESSMENT FOR LEARNING

Quality pre-school experiences enhance a child's learning and development, and early childhood is a critical time for such development (Thurtle, 1997). If doing nothing is an unacceptable option, what should we be doing? In many ways identification is inextricably linked to assessment. Many people spend huge amounts of time checking to see that children have 'learned' a predetermined set of skills that will ensure they make a good start at 'formal' school. By doing this, educators can identify the gaps that exist and seek to plug these through extra practice, homework and one-to-one tuition. The effect of this kind of assessment on learning and individuals is neatly described in a story told to me by a nursery teacher:

> *It's June in the nursery and for the past week and a half I have spent my time walking around with a red clipboard 'testing' children, particularly in mathematics and language, recording results and completing forms for the 'big' school. I walked over to a table where a nursery nurse and four children were working on an activity. I was in fact going to ask the nursery nurse if she had watched a particular programme on TV the night before. On approaching the table with my red clipboard one of the children turned to look at me. On seeing the red clipboard he looked up into my face and said confidently 'it's red and it's a triangle'.*
>
> (Nursery teacher)

Perhaps some of the traditional forms of assessment that exist are unhelpful. With the number of ticks required on, for example, Foundation Stage assessment in England, one can well imagine the above scenario happening. While this true story probably brought a smile to your face, it strikes me as a sad indictment on our education systems if that is the first reaction of a four-year-old to the approach of an adult in the early years setting.

However, assessment can be quite different. It is more helpful to find out what children can learn with help and support rather than simply testing what they have already learned. Assessment that supports the learning process can help to challenge gifted and talented learners, extending their learning rather than merely giving them more of something they are already good at. Indeed, a new approach to the assessment of all children will benefit those who are gifted and talented and help us to identify emerging abilities. It will also help us to meet the requirements expected of us by our various education systems.

Margaret Carr (2001) suggests that we need to rethink assessment. We need to focus on learning instead of the idea that there is a predetermined set of skills or that there is predetermined knowledge that a child must possess. The old style of assessment she has called a 'folk model' of assessment. In other words, it is a set of beliefs about assessment that have grown and developed over the years with no one challenging them or questioning the rationale for them. She suggests we need to move towards an 'alternative model' of assessment where the learners' understanding is arrived at by collaboration between the adult and the learner (see Table 2.1).

Table 2.1 **Assumption in two models of assessment: a folk model and an alternative**

Assumptions about	Folk model of assessment	An alternative model of assessment
Purpose	To check against a shortlist of skills that describe 'competence' at school entry	To enhance learning
Outcome of interest	Fragmented and context-free school-oriented skills	Learning dispositions
Focus of intervention	Deficit, gap-filling, is foregrounded	Credit, disposition enhancing, is foregrounded
Validity	Objective observation	Interpreted observations, discussions and agreements
Progress	Hierarchies of skills	Increasingly complex participation
Procedures	Checklists	Learning stories
Value to practitioners	Surveillance by external agencies	For communicating with four audiences: children, families, other staff and self (the practitioner)

Reprinted by permission of Sage Publications Ltd from Margaret Carr, Assessment in Early Childhood Settings, copyright Margaret Carr 2001.

In the folk model the following may happen. Staff in the early years setting draw up a checklist of predetermined skills that children will undertake. Successful completion of these tasks will indicate that a child is ready to move on to the next task or is ready to start 'formal' school, etc. These tasks are likely to be familiar to you and might include:

- colouring in within the lines (i.e. 'neatly')

- using scissors (without looking as though they might stab themselves or someone else)

- writing their name independently (e.g. on their art work)

- recognising numbers (e.g. from environmental print)

- reciting the numbers 1–20 and beyond

- knowing some letter and sound names (e.g. 'what sound does your name begin with?)

- knowing which way to hold a book (when in the library corner)

- knowing how to turn over the pages of a book

- knowing that print reads from left to right.

These tasks may be explicitly taught and they will almost certainly be tested. There will be an assumption that children must be able to complete these tasks with ease before moving on to other skills. Indeed there will be an assumption that learning will be difficult and may even be hindered if a child is unable to complete these apparently basic and crucial skills. These tasks can be neatly ticked off on a list, the information can be passed on to formal school and there may be assumptions that these children will 'do well' as they progress through the education system. I am not arguing here that these 'skills' are not important; however, I am saying that we cannot look at them in isolation and we cannot say that a child who is proficient at these things is necessarily gifted and talented.

How then, do we make these changes to assessment? In the 'alternative model' of assessment the following may occur. Staff in the early years setting will:

- find out what children already know, understand and can do

- discuss with children what the learning goals are for the activity

- discuss with children what they have done well and what they need to work on, and what they put their progress down to

- allow children to experiment with resources

- look for children who persist with a task

- encourage children to express points of view and emotions.

Children who demonstrate these abilities may also score very well on our previous list, but being proficient in the dispositions in the alternative model is, in the longer term, more beneficial as the child enters formal school. These dispositions are a firm grounding for meaningful lifelong learning and not simply a list of tasks proving they are skilled at 'hoop jumping'. However, these kinds of 'dispositions' do not lend themselves to an accountability-based approach to learning. They don't fit neatly into a checklist or tick-box culture. But they are extremely important if we believe that learning is not about a single end point rather a multiplicity of end points. In other words, end points are made up of a number of dispositions with no one being more important than the other – the *process* is as important as the *product*. If it is important to staff and parents that things are neat, tidy, ordered and as near perfect as possible then this suggested change of emphasis from 'product to process' may well be difficult. Full explanations of the shift in emphasis in assessment should be given to all before embarking on such a change – this will avoid a clash of expectations and possibly difficult parent meetings. Just as I am suggesting we need to share with children what the learning goals are for the activity, so we need to share our learning goals with parents. We are all learners, and what is good for one set of learners is good for another.

- Assessment should lead to better learning experiences, not just tick lists.

- The alternative model of assessment offers meaningful learning experiences.

- Learning is 'messy'; a linear approach to learning should be avoided.

- There is no one end point to learning; learning is an assortment of end points.

- Process should be more important than product.

- Parents need to understand the 'alternative model' of assessment.

BUILDING UP A PICTURE

If we adopt this so-called alternative model of assessment then it is vital that we build up a picture of the child that comprises as much information as possible. Our 'one checklist or tick list', while useful, will only supply some information, it won't tell us all we need to know about the child.

It would seem that gathering data from a variety of sources would allow us to build up an holistic picture of the child which might be helpful. This data would come from the following sources:

- observation in the early years setting

- the children themselves

- parents

- peers.

Let's build up a picture of a young gifted and talented learner, called Anna, as we go along. We can then use this example to see how we can take forward Anna's learning.

Observation in the early years setting

Not all adults working with young children will be involved in formal observation of the children. However, all will be observing and making judgements on a daily basis. Indeed, educators often complain of spending so much time observing that they have no time to work with the children. However, structured, purposeful observation is a vital tool for the educator. Through observation we can not only monitor young children and their learning, but we can monitor our own actions and reactions to situations.

If we are going to observe then we have to be clear about what we are looking for. But herein lies a difficulty. Often we have in mind very clear aims for each activity and often these are shaped by national documentation. If we have very precise goals and learning outcomes then that is what we'll focus on and there is a real danger that we will miss the vital learning that is taking place because we are so focused on particular outcomes.

A 'tracking of achievement' sheet would allow us to gather information that will be useful for our final 'big picture'. Over time these sheets can be completed during a variety of activities, allowing a profile to be built up of individual children. They could be kept in a central file allowing open access and can be added to by anyone who sees something significant. Areas to be commented on would include:

- questioning

- understanding

- creativity

- logical thinking

- remembering

- working with others

- taking risks.

While these areas are not an exhaustive list, they are a starting point for the observation of gifted and talented learners. An example of such a sheet is given in Table 2.2, and there is a blank template that you can photocopy.

| Table 2.2 | Example observation sheet |

TRACKING ACHIEVEMENT

Name of child: Anna

Category	Observation
Questioning	• Asks questions • Goes into details when answering questions
Understanding	• Demonstrates strong opinions/feelings • Extracts inferences
Creativity	• Inventor • Creates a new design • Is extremely inquisitive • Has 'madcap', impractical ideas
Logical thinking	• Thrives on complex activities
Remembering	• Is keenly observant • Manipulates information
Working with others	• Prefers to talk with adults
Takes risks	• Good at guessing but has to be encouraged to do so
Additional information	• Anna likes to get things right and isn't happy when made to have a go at something or when she thinks there's a chance she will 'get it wrong'.

OBSERVATION

TRACKING ACHIEVEMENT

Name of child:

Category	Observation
Questioning	
Understanding	
Creativity	
Logical thinking	
Remembering	
Working with others	
Takes risks	
Additional information	

The child

Young gifted and talented children will know they can do certain things. Their families are often amazed at some of the things they can do and often the children themselves notice that they are good at things and can do things their friends can't. Often they know they can do things that their key workers and teachers didn't know they could do. Sometimes that's because they don't get a chance to show these individuals what they can do. Let's think about this from Anna's perspective.

The library corner

Anna always gets excited when her key worker asks her to go to the library corner. She loves all kinds of books and likes nothing better than sitting on the big chair and reading a story. The only problem is that the key worker always reads the story to her. She loves having someone read a story to her, especially at bedtime, but she also likes reading a story for herself. She never really gets a chance to do that in the early years setting. They always sit in their groups and listen to the key worker and answer questions that the key worker asks. Her key worker knows she knows about words and books because she can answer all the questions he/she asks but sometimes Anna has questions about the book too but she doesn't often get the chance to ask her questions. It's good that the children know about authors and illustrators and rhyming words and which way to turn the pages, but Anna wants to know why the author wrote the story that way or why the illustrator chose that colour or why the story ended the way it did – she never gets a chance to ask these kind of questions.

Anna has highlighted a number of issues particularly related to reading for us:

- Young children are not always offered an opportunity to 'read' books for themselves.
- Discussions are usually adult-led.
- Children have questions but are not always offered opportunities to ask these questions.
- In an effort to ensure that we cover the basic knowledge required for literacy activities, we tend to focus on certain aspects of literacy which again are adult-led.

While not all children will be ready to participate at the level suggested by Anna, those who are, are being denied the opportunity to do so. While Anna has highlighted issues related to language and reading in particular, the same issues apply to all curricular areas.

One of the problems is that key workers ask questions about activities children do in the early years setting. So they say things like:

- How many ducks can you see in the picture?

- What are you going to put in that bit?

- How can you make your model move?

- Did you make that by yourself?

There's nothing wrong with these questions but some children have lots of thoughts in their heads about things they can do or questions they want to ask and they don't often get a chance to talk to adults about them.

Children may tell us they like listening to music. Of course they will listen to music in the early years setting but as the educator we may not know that children like listening to music at home. Armed with this knowledge, the educator can take time to talk to the children about music and to find out what kind of music they like to listen to.

Because life in the early years setting is busy and activities are often tightly organised and timetabled, we frequently miss opportunities to find out about the children and their interests and abilities. Sometimes this is because we don't ask questions about the wider world of the children. We focus on early years events and activities and often these are linked to assessment and attainment and the predetermined sets of knowledge and skills discussed earlier.

- Activities should not become adult driven.

- Allow time for children to ask their own questions.

- Focus on wider aspects of learning such as attitude and motivation.

I asked some young gifted and talented learners what they were good at and what they enjoyed. It was interesting to discover that some children enjoyed things they did not perceive themselves to be particularly good at, while others were good at things they did not necessarily enjoy. This idea of the enjoyment of a task is interesting. When we enjoy something we are much more likely to participate. This disparity between enjoyment and competence could possibly lead to the label 'underachiever' being given when perhaps the child simply did not 'enjoy' the activity. This is worth being aware of and watching out for. Asking questions will help you to do this.

Here is a sample of the kind of answers you might record when talking with a child. There is also a blank version for you to photocopy.

Children's interests and abilities

Name Anna

1. What kind of things do you enjoy doing?

numbers		music	yes	exploring	
words	yes	art	yes	experimenting	
reading	yes	talking	yes	other	yes
sports		listening	yes		

If you said 'other' or something else, can you tell me a bit more about what it is you like doing?

> Acting out stories. I like to be the characters in the story. My favourite is when I can be a princess. I like dressing up and dancing too.

2. What do you feel you are really good at?

numbers		music		exploring	
words	yes	art		experimenting	
reading	yes	talking	yes	other	yes
sports		listening			

If you said 'other' or something else, can you tell me a bit more about what it is you are really good at?

> I'm really good at speaking out loud, like when we have to introduce something at the concert.

3. Have we helped you to become better at what you are good at?

Yes [yes]   No [ ]

4. If yes, how have we helped you?

> I got to introduce the song at the Christmas concert.

5. How do you know you're really good at doing something?

My mum and/or dad told me	yes	My friends told me	
A relative told me		I worked it out for myself	yes
My key worker told me	yes	Some other way	

6. Do you think there are others here who are good at the same things as you?

Yes [ ]   No [no]

7. Would you like to work with someone who was good at the same things as you?

Yes [yes]   No [ ]

These questions offer a starting point for engaging young children in conversation and recording their answers. You will be able to think of many more questions but these should get you started. You should note that all children can be asked these questions and not just those that you 'think' might be gifted and talented.

Children's interests and abilities

Name _____

1. What kind of things do you enjoy doing?

numbers		music		exploring	
words		art		experimenting	
reading		talking		other	
sports		listening			

If you said 'other' or something else, can you tell me a bit more about what it is you like doing?

2. What do you feel you are really good at?

numbers		music		exploring	
words		art		experimenting	
reading		talking		other	
sports		listening			

If you said 'other' or something else, can you tell me a bit more about what it is you are really good at?

3. Have we helped you to become better at what you are good at?

Yes [ ]   No [ ]

4. If yes, how have we helped you?

5. How do you know you're really good at doing something?

My mum and/or dad told me		My friends told me	
A relative told me		I worked it out for myself	
People at my nursery told me		Some other way	

6. Do you think there are others here who are good at the same things as you?

Yes [ ]   No [ ]

7. Would you like to work with someone who was good at the same things as you?

Yes [ ]   No [ ]

Gathering this kind of information allows you to begin to build up a picture of the child from the child's perspective. Engaging with children in conversation about their likes and dislikes and their abilities can make them feel a valued and important member of the early years setting. Remember that in Chapter 1 I argued that children use feedback from significant others to build up a personal theory relating to intelligence. You are a 'significant other' in the young child's life and showing this interest in them and their abilities will mean a lot to them.

- Take time just to 'talk' to the children.
- Know about the children's lives outside of the early years setting.
- Value the contributions each child can make to life in the early years setting.
- Use the information you have about children to plan their learning experiences.

Parents

Parents are often the source of valuable information for early years settings. They know the child better than anyone and see the child in different circumstances. They have much to contribute to the overall picture of a child and their abilities. However, often parents are viewed with suspicion. 'Every parent in my establishment would think their child is gifted' is a view sometimes expressed by educators. While undoubtedly difficulties arise when parents have unrealistically high expectations for their children, to ignore their opinions is equally dangerous. Often parents are reluctant to tell educators about their child's ability, as they fear they will be perceived as 'pushy' or 'prejudiced'. I asked some parents of older gifted and talented children to name one thing that they would have liked educators to do when their child was young. All the parents answered 'I wish they had believed me when I said my child had abilities'. Early years settings need to ensure that they create an ethos that allows parents to share information.

Such an ethos could be created by:

- being welcoming and friendly
- actively listening to parents
- sharing information with parents
- believing what parents tell you
- wanting to work in partnership with parents.

If a parent indicates that they think their child might have particular abilities, it can be useful to find out a little more about these abilities. One way to do this would be to ask parents to complete a short questionnaire. Alternatively the questionnaire could be used as the basis for discussion and interview. The following sample questionnaire illustrates the kind of information you might record. Again, we also provide a photocopiable template. The questionnaire itself offers initial questions that will provide some information and act as a starter for discussion.

Information from parents

Name of child Anna

1. At what age did you begin to think that your child had particular abilities? Please put an X in the appropriate box.

0–12months		12–18 months	
18 months–24 months	X	2–3 years	
3–5 years		5+ years	

2. Were you the first to notice your child's abilities?

Yes [ ]   No [no]

If no, please state who first noticed and what they noticed

The health visitor. She was surprised Anna was asking about letters and knew sounds of letters at such an early age.

3. In what area/s do your child's abilities lie?

music	yes	reading	yes
mathematics	yes	talking	yes
art		physical, e.g. sports, dance	
language	yes	good with people	yes
languages		science	
drama	yes	other/s	

If other/s, please state which _____

Further details/information about my child's abilities

> Anna seems to have a very lively imagination. She is always dressing up and pretending to be a character from the book she is reading. She likes to talk with adults but then she spends a lot of time around adults. Her granny looks after her when I'm at work and she doesn't really have any younger cousins or relatives. She has started going to dancing and the teacher says she has very good rhythm and remembers the steps from one week to the next. She's always got her nose in a book. She also likes to watch television by turning down the sound and reading the subtitles.

4. As a parent, how do you encourage, challenge and stretch your child's abilities at home?

   Attend club/organisation

   Buy resources to support my child

   Use the computer/internet

   Talk to my child

   Take my child on outings/visits that relate to her ability

   Other

   > I like to try to make sure that Anna gets lots of opportunities to try things and not just things she's good at. However, we do go to the library three times a week.

5. What could we do to work together with you to challenge and encourage your child?

   > I'm quite happy with what you are doing at the moment although I do worry a bit about what will happen when she goes to school. I don't want her to be bored.

Thank you for completing this questionnaire.

Information from parents

Name of child _____

Please put an X in the appropriate box.

1. At what age did you begin to think that your child had particular abilities?

    0–12months [ ]   12–18 months [ ]

    18 months–24 months [ ]   2–3 years [ ]

    3–5 years [ ]   5+ years [ ]

2. Were you the first to notice your child's abilities?

    Yes [ ]   No [ ]

    If no, please state who first noticed and what they noticed

    [   ]

3. In what area/s do your child's abilities lie?

music		reading	
mathematics		talking	
art		physical, e.g. sports, dance	
language		good with people	
languages		science	
drama		other/s	

If other/s, please state which _____

Further details/information about my child's abilities

```

```

4. As a parent, how do you encourage, challenge and stretch your child's abilities at home?

Attend club/organisation ☐

Buy resources to support my child ☐

Use the computer/internet ☐

Talk to my child ☐

Take my child on outings/visits that relate to his/her ability ☐

Other

```

```

5. What could we do to work together with you to challenge and encourage your child?

```

```

Thank you for completing this questionnaire.

Peers

Gardner (1983) would argue that being good with other people and knowing about yourself are intelligences that need to be recognised, nurtured and developed. Anyone working with young children will know that mostly they are interested in 'themselves' first and foremost. This 'egocentric' approach to life is part of growing up and development. I have witnessed young children making very hurtful comments to one another – 'you're really stupid', 'you're being silly'. If young children can make these kinds of judgement about their peers, then they may well be capable of making more positive judgements about their peers too. To see if children had the ability to think wider than themselves, I tried asking young children: 'who would be good at helping me with certain activities in the early years setting?' Answers to these types of questions allow us to see how young children view their peers and give us an insight into their stage of interaction. The answers to my questions broadly fell into three categories:

1. Me – I would be good at helping you.

2. Me and my friend would be good at helping you.

3. My friend would be good at helping you.

The first category of answer was most common among the children.

For example:

Staff:	Who would be a good person to help me with jigsaws?
Child:	Me
Staff:	Who would be a good person to help me cut out shapes?
Child:	Me

Reasons for this may include:

- they were not ready to 'see beyond themselves'

- they are trying to establish 'goodness and badness' and they wanted me to know how good they were (this links to the work of Carol Dweck, which was outlined in Chapter 1).

The second category of answer suggests some awareness of others and their abilities in the early years setting and often the other names included those in their friendship group. For example:

Staff:	Who would be a good person to help me with jigsaws?
Child:	Me and my friend
Staff:	Who would be a good person to help me cut out shapes?
Child:	Me and my two friends

Children who were 'very able' most commonly gave the third category of answer in a range of areas, e.g. motor control, language, number, art, etc. They were also all very articulate. They demonstrated a level of understanding about their peers and themselves not seen in the other children. They also offered an explanation for their choice of name, almost as though they were providing evidence for their choice. For example:

Staff:	Who would be a good person to help me with jigsaws?
Child:	Frida, she's very good at jigsaws and I'm quite good too
Staff:	Who would be a good person to help me cut out shapes?
Child:	Stuart, he cuts very carefully

In answer to this last question, one child also replied 'that would have to be me, I'm definitely the best at cutting out in this nursery!' While the child being questioned still featured in the answers, there did not appear to be the same need to be 'first' and they also demonstrated an ability to reflect and think about the answer before giving a name. While the friends of the children I interviewed featured in their answers, they included other children in the early years setting and appeared more aware of the larger group.

Asking questions will give you the opportunity to gauge where children are in their development. It will also allow you to begin to build up a social picture of the early years setting. You will see friendship groups emerging. Don't be surprised when undertaking this activity if you discover that not all the children know each other's names. It never ceases to amaze me how often we take this for granted and yet closer inspection often reveals that a child can tell you what another child is good at but not their name – 'him, the boy with the red jumper, he's good at football!'

The following pages offer a framework for questioning. The questions have tried to take into account a range of curricular areas and skills including:

- fine motor skills
- motor development
- musical ability
- emotional intelligence
- mathematical ability
- reading
- communication and language.

You will be able to add to this list and adapt it so that it fits the requirements of your early years setting. A sample shows you the kind of answers you might be given as you discuss this with the children. There is a blank template for you to photocopy.

Who is good at what? – some questions to get you started

Sit with the child in a quieter area of the early years setting. Use the following script to help you frame the scene.

Adult: I've got lots of jobs that need to be done and I want to try to find girls and boys who could help me do these jobs. I'm going to tell you what I need done and then ask you who you think would be a good person to do this job. Perhaps you think more than one person might be good at this job. If you do, that's OK.

Name of child Anna:

Question	Nomination
If I couldn't finish a jigsaw, who would I ask to help me?	Jemma and Hope
Who would I ask to help me cut out shapes?	Jack
Who would I choose to be in my sports team?	Kwaku
Who should I choose to sing my favourite song?	Rachael
If I fell and hurt myself, who would be good to take care of me?	Jack and me
If I had to do some counting and needed help, whom would I ask?	Robin
Who should I choose to paint my picture?	Me
If I had to choose someone to read a book with me, whom should I choose?	Me
If I had to pick someone to speak to the boys and girls, whom should I choose?	Me
If I had to choose someone to play an instrument, whom should I choose?	Hope and me
If I needed someone to solve a puzzle, whom should I choose?	Robin
If I needed someone to talk to, who would be a good friend?	Jordan and me

Who is good at what? – some questions to get you started

Sit with the child in a quieter area of the early years setting.
Use the following script to help you frame the scene.

Adult: I've got lots of jobs that need done and I want to try to find girls and boys who could help me do these jobs. I'm going to tell you what I need done and then ask you who you think would be a good person to do this job. Perhaps you think more than one person might be good at this job. If you do, that's OK.

Name of child:

Question	Nomination
If I couldn't finish a jigsaw, who would I ask to help me?	
Who would I ask to help me cut out shapes?	
Who would I choose to be in my sports team?	
Who should I choose to sing my favourite song?	
If I fell and hurt myself, who would be good to take care of me?	
If I had to do some counting and needed help, whom would I ask?	
Who should I choose to paint my picture?	
If I had to choose someone to read a book with me, whom should I choose?	
If I had to pick someone to speak to the boys and girls, whom should I choose?	
If I had to choose someone to play an instrument, whom should I choose?	
If I needed someone to solve a puzzle, whom should I choose?	
If I needed someone to talk to, who would be a good friend?	

- Include the child in the data-gathering process.
- Value the views of parents.
- Offer parents an opportunity to share their views.
- Involve all the children in the identification process.
- Be interesed in how the children learn, not just what they produce.

PULLING IT ALL TOGETHER

You have gathered data from four sources:

- observation

- the child

- the parent

- peers.

It's important to look at it all and to decide what it is telling you. One way to do this is to identify four key things from each source that you think are important and note them on a 'Big Picture' sheet. Having noted them on this summary sheet, you will begin to get an overall picture of the child and their abilities. From this you can start to decide how you can challenge the child to develop these abilities further through the activities easily made available in the early years setting.

Having taken Anna as an example, we know some things about her already but if we put our knowledge together and link it to national UK documentation, what does the big picture suggest we need to be doing? The following sample sheet shows us what we already know. A blank photocopiable template follows.

The big picture

Name of child: Anna
Name/s of staff: Mina

Observation	Key points
	1. manipulates information
	2. thrives on complex activities
	3. goes into detail, expands
	4. initiates tasks
Parents	Key points
	1. been asking about sounds and letters from an early age
	2. reads all the time
	3. turns down the sound on TV and reads the subtitles
	4. often visits the library
Child	Key points
	1. enjoys language-related activities
	2. is really good at reading
	3. would like to work with others
	4. has a good self-awareness
Peers	Key points
	1. has a wide range of friends
	2. can appreciate others' abilities
	3. can identify abilities in others
	4. strong interpersonal skills

The big picture

Name of child:
Name/s of staff:

Observation	Key points
	1.
	2.
	3.
	4.
Parents	Key points
	1.
	2.
	3.
	4.
Child	Key points
	1.
	2.
	3.
	4.
Peers	Key points
	1.
	2.
	3.
	4.

This overview can then be used to plan learning experiences for children. At this point of course, we have to consider national UK documentation. In some countries there is a national curriculum that must be followed; in other countries there are guidelines that are there to help frame the learning experience. Closer examination of this documentation would suggest that there are broadly similar outcomes for early years education across the four nations that make up the UK.

Having looked at Anna, let's now look at the documentation and see how we can use it plus the knowledge we now have of her to plan accordingly.

NATIONAL UK DOCUMENTATION

Scotland, Northern Ireland, England and Wales all have their own education systems and accompanying legislation, documentation and approach to gifted and talented education. So what does the documentation say? Stories and story telling has played an important part in our past. Universally, children like listening to stories. Let's take as an example the idea of listening to stories and rhymes and see what documentation has to say (Table 2.3).

Table 2.3 National UK documentation

Learning outcomes (England)	Learning outcomes (Scotland)
NLS Early Learning Goals Listen to favourite nursery rhymes, stories and songs. Join in with repeated refrains, anticipating key events and important phrases.	*3–5 Curriculum Framework* Communication and language Listen with enjoyment and respond to stories, songs, music, rhymes and other poetry. Listen and respond to the sounds and rhythm of words in stories, songs, music and rhymes. Recognise the link between the written and spoken word.
Learning outcomes (Northern Ireland)	**Desirable outcomes (Wales)**
Foundation Stage: Talking and listening Listening and responding: children should have opportunities to listen and respond to a wide range of stories, songs, poems including audio tapes and writing of other children. Listening and remembering: children should have the opportunities to learn rhymes and number rhymes, etc. Developing an awareness of sounds: children should have opportunities to develop an awareness of rhyming words.	*Language, literacy and communication* Listen to a good story. Listen, respond to and recall songs, nursery rhymes, poems and jingles. Ask questions and listen to responses.

As you read these, you can begin to see the common experiences that children across the UK share in their education – listening, talking, remembering, responding to a variety of rhymes, etc. Given these similarities I would suggest that, regardless of the documentation and legislation available in the individual home nations, good educational experiences throughout the UK will seek to:

- find out what children already know, understand and can do

- discuss with children what the learning goals are for the activity

- discuss with children what they have done well and what they need to work on, and what they put their progress down to.

If this sounds familiar then it should come as no surprise. This is the same as was suggested in our alternative model of assessment earlier in this chapter. This, along with what we know about good learning opportunities should allow us to offer real challenge to children. A key theme of the UK documentation relates to how children respond to stories. What might this mean for Anna? We need to ask ourselves some additional questions:

- How does she respond to stories at the moment?

- What do we want her to be able to do next?

- Have we shared our ideas with her?

The national documentation in each country can be very helpful in ensuring that children are challenged, that learning is fun and that attainment is raised.

Using information gathered from a variety of sources alongside national documentation will allow us to offer appropriate and challenging activities for young children. Let's relate that next to particular curricular areas.

SUMMING UP

Some key points about the identification of gifted and talented learners have been made in this chapter.

- Labels for children are not always necessary, but challenging learning experiences are.

- Assessment should be about learning rather than simply plugging gaps in knowledge and skills.

- We need to build up the whole picture of the child's abilities and interests.

- The information we gather along with national documentation can help us to plan next steps and challenging learning experiences.

Chapter 3

Activities and resources

This chapter will consider:

- the cross-curricular nature of problem-solving.

- the common resources and activities on offer across four specific curricular areas.

- the skills and abilities gifted and talented children might present in each of these curricular areas.

So far we have looked at how to gather information about children's abilities from four main sources:

- observation in the early years setting

- the children themselves

- parents

- peers.

To focus our attention on aspects of learning we will now think about particular curricular areas and what young children might be doing during various activities. We will consider four curricular areas:

- physical movement/motor development

- music

- language

- mathematics.

While this chapter suggests advanced responses that young children might demonstrate, I am in no way suggesting that they can automatically be labelled 'gifted and talented'. What I am suggesting is that if this is what they can do already, then we need to be aware of this and decide how we will challenge them next time they arrive at the gym, the music corner or wherever.

> Competence in the activities and skills listed in this chapter are examples only and does not necessarily mean a child should be labelled gifted and talented. It does mean that they need to be challenged.

PHYSICAL MOVEMENT/MOTOR DEVELOPMENT

Why physical movement and motor development?

- Children from all countries and cultures engage in physical activity.

- Children enjoy physical activities and many would rather engage in this than other kinds of tasks.

- Children's health and general well-being can be enhanced through physical activities.

- Children's development in these areas can positively influence other forms of learning.

It has been suggested in the media that, in the UK, we are not doing enough to develop the talents and abilities of young athletes. Much discussion about this issue took place during the 2004 Olympic Games in Athens. Neglecting physical movement and motor development and children who show particular ability in this area is likely to impact not only on the United Kingdom's medal-winning chances at future Olympic Games but on the development of children generally – physically, emotionally and academically. Coupled with the growing concern over childhood obesity, can we really afford to neglect this vital aspect of the curriculum?

Young children love to move. Indeed, they spend much of their time moving and yet this important aspect of their development is all too easily overlooked as we focus on the important areas of numeracy and literacy skills. The significance of motor development in relation to learning generally should not be underestimated. Competence in physical movement and motor development will greatly enhance learning across the curriculum.

Motor development in the early years is primarily concerned with:

- improving coordination

- control

- manipulation

- movement.

There are some key skills in all of this that the educator will be looking for when working with children.

A starting point for consideration is how well developed the children's fine and gross motor skills are. In other words, how well do they make small and big movements? Competence in these areas will offer a strong starting place for future work in a range of curricular areas. Children who are gifted and talented in physical activities may well present highly developed skills and abilities relating to physical movement and motor development.

So what will these children be able to do? Generally, when looking for competence in **fine motor skills**, children will be able to easily complete the following tasks:

- fasten and unfasten buttons on their clothes/buckles on their shoes

- cut out shapes using scissors

- colour within lines

- rotate their palms upwards/downwards

- attempt to tie their shoe laces

- use a knife and fork when eating

- touch each finger with their thumb (right and left hands)

- build a tower of bricks.

It can be seen how several of these skills, for example colouring within lines, will be detected in other curricular areas. However, the trick for the educator is to use these skills in a cross-curricular manner and to see the relationship between colouring in and physical movement and motor development and then to challenge children in all areas.

Generally, when looking for competence in **gross motor skills**, children will be able to easily complete the following tasks:

- hop just as well on both legs

- gallop with the left or the right foot in front

- balance on one leg without wobbling about for 5 seconds

- use a heel-to-toe action, walk along a straight line

- bounce a large ball with one hand

- catch a large ball each time with both hands

- jump and land with both feet together

- stop and start quickly when travelling round a space

- curve, curl and stretch out the body

- run around in a large space without bumping into anyone or anything.

These skills underpin many aspects of physical movement and motor development. While there are many approaches to physical movement and motor development, we are going to concentrate on skills. The development of skills is important, not only for those who may be gifted and talented, but for all young children in our care.

Let's think about the activities we offer in our early years setting. We will consider what we might see children doing during certain activities and we will also consider what children, already proficient in particular skills will be doing. We will look at five common activities and their related resources in an early years setting:

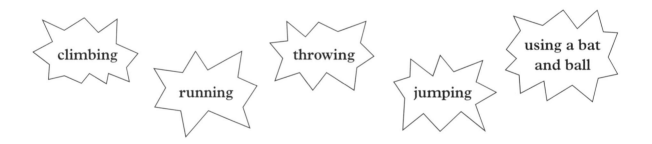

climbing running throwing jumping using a bat and ball

◉ Climbing

Even before they can walk, young children are using climbing actions to pull themselves along the floor or onto furniture. Young children also have a fascination for stairs and will experiment by clambering up and down stairs with bottoms in the air and much effort being expended. Often when left to play, young children will climb up fences, walls and trees. This desire to climb often leaves parents and educators alike holding their breath. However, in an early years setting there are controlled opportunities to develop this natural ability and curiosity.

The climbing frame, whether outdoors or indoors, offers wonderful opportunities for gross motor development. With guidance and support, children can become confident climbers.

Resource: Climbing apparatus

Activity/resources	Responses	Advanced responses
Climbing, e.g. on apparatus	• be nervous when using the equipment and perhaps even be reluctant to join in • take great effort to hold body weight • be erratic and hesitant when climbing • use same arm/leg action • have a weak grasp of the bars	• have confidence on apparatus • hold body weight with ease • display effortless, flowing movements as they climb • use opposite arm/leg action • have a strong grasp of the bars

Running

When faced with a large open space, young children zoom around, often shrieking and screaming with delight as the wind whips through their hair. The whole body is involved in running – arms to propel them forward, long steps to cover ground quickly. Running with purpose and control takes some degree of skill and young children can often be seen running so fast that they can't stop. It is the educators' job to support children and help them to experience the joy of running.

Resource: large spaces

Activity/resources	Responses	Advanced responses
Running	• overstated lean • uncoordinated action • flailing leg and arm movement • head forward • not in the air much during the running process • lower leg 'flaps' about	• bent forwards • flowing action • leg and arm movements in opposition to each other • during the running process the runner is in the air • the supporting leg is firm and extended

Throwing

From an early age children throw things. Frequently they may throw away something they don't want, e.g. their soft toy. At first the throw can be 'floppy' with little control over where the object lands or the distance it is thrown. Later the throw can be more deliberate and controlled – such as when a child is throwing something away in a temper, the object may be thrown at someone or something to reinforce a point and communicate how the child is feeling. There should of course be a more positive reason for throwing something, such as when we play with a ball. There are three main ways of throwing an object:

- underarm

- overarm

- sideways.

Each throw has a specific purpose; e.g. overarm would be the choice for throwing something a distance. The educator can work with young children to help them acquire greater accuracy in throwing and help them to select the right throw for the activity. There is also ample opportunity for the educator to discuss when you should throw something and the safety aspects involved in throwing objects.

Resources: Large balls, beanbags, small balls, quoits

Activity/resources	Responses	Advanced responses
Throwing, e.g. overarm throw	• very little backswing • poor transference of weight • non-throwing arm hangs limply at side • steps forward on same leg as throwing arm • child has difficulty releasing the object in the correct direction	• arm swings back prior to throw • weight transfers forwards • non-throwing arm is held out to aid balance • steps forward on opposite foot to throwing arm • throwing arm follows through towards the direction of the throw

Jumping

Young children can often be seen jumping up and down with excitement. Jumping into the air from one foot or two feet and landing again on one foot or two feet requires some degree of control. In fact, often the landing is the tricky bit for young children and frequently a jump ends with a child wobbling and losing his/her balance. The educator can work with the child to overcome these difficulties thus ensuring, among other things, a safe landing.

Resource: Flat space

Activity/resources	Responses	Advanced responses
Jumping, e.g. a vertical jump	• no preparation before jumping • no 'push' through the legs • body remains curled and bent when in the air • awkward landing, often losing balance	• squat down prior to jumping • legs extend and stretch • body is fully stretched when in the air • controlled landing with knees and ankles bent

Using a bat and ball

This is perhaps one of the most difficult skills to perform. When using a bat and ball a number of skills come into play at one time. For example, hand–eye coordination is essential, especially when this involves using an object other than a part of the body. Being able to focus on a ball as it travels through the air and track it until it makes contact with the bat is also a highly developed skill. For some children these skills will develop as they mature and progress through the education system. A structured programme can support children as they develop.

Resources: Various size balls, various size bats

Activity/resources	Responses	Advanced responses
Using a bat and ball	• does not prepare to hit the ball • body faces the front • stance does not alter • eyes do not make contact with the ball • bat 'stabs' at ball	• bat is in position to receive the ball • body faces the side in preparation • weight is moved to front foot • eyes follow the ball through the air • bat hits ball with sweeping action

MUSIC

Why music?

- From birth, young children take part in vocal play.

- First musical experiences are known to shape future interest in music.

- Music allows children to express and develop their feelings and emotions.

- There are links between musical development and development in the other creative media, e.g. word/sound rhythms, syllables.

- Making music, both individually and collectively, is good fun.

- Music provides an ideal opportunity for listening for sound and word patterns in a fun way.

- Music develops memory skills.

Music is often an area in which educators lack confidence. They claim they 'can't sing a note' or are 'tone deaf'. Consequently, depending on the ability and confidence of staff in the early years setting, music is paid scant attention. However, we know that music is important for aspects of human development. Music is all around us – on TV, on radio, in supermarkets. Music is used to create atmosphere and is a powerful tool for communicating our emotions.

As educators we have a responsibility to nurture music-making. By doing this we will encourage children to build up their musical confidence and may well do the same for the adults involved.

Let's think about the activities we offer in our early years setting. We will consider what we might see children doing during certain activities and we will also consider what children, who are already proficient, will be doing. We will look at some common activities and their related resources in an early years setting:

Singing

Singing is a natural expression for humans. Babies gurgle and babble and we know that they respond to songs with a strong beat. Young children appear to enjoy singing familiar songs over and over again. They experiment with their voices and often begin to gain confidence in singing aloud. While the repetition of songs is helpful, young children also relish the opportunity to learn new songs and this offers the early years educator the possibility of drawing on the wealth of materials around.

Resources: Nursery rhymes, action songs, counting songs, echo songs, tapes, CDs

Activity/resources	Responses	Advanced responses
Singing a song. 'Okki Tokki Unga': Action Songs for Children; Apusskidu: Songs for Children; Mango Spice: 44 Caribbean Songs; Tongo: Count Me In: 44 Songs and Rhymes about Numbers; Tom Thumb's Musical Maths: Developing Maths Skills with Simple Songs; etc.	● don't participate ● show no interest ● easily distracted ● poor memory for words ● monotone ● don't recognise familiar songs	● enthusiastic ● responds to activities ● can hold a tune ● makes up songs ● enjoys performing ● recognises familiar songs in varying contexts, e.g. on TV

● Instruments and sound-making

Babies begin to explore sound when, for example, they shake their rattle. They discover that different rattles produce different sounds. As they become older and progress to such things as banging pots and pans, they also begin to realise that not only do different pots produce different sounds but also that the sounds produced are not always welcomed by the adults around them. The adults often tightly control the playing of instruments and other sound-making equipment in the early years setting. This may inhibit creativity and exploration. Young children need time to develop this aspect of music making.

Resources: Tuned percussion instruments, e.g. chime bars, hand chimes, piano; untuned percussion, e.g. drums, woodblocks, bells, shakers, triangles, cymbals, tambourines

Activity/resources	Responses	Advanced responses
Instruments and sound-making	● has to be shown each time how to hold and play the instrument ● plays the instrument erratically ● plays the instrument at inappropriate times	● remembers how to hold and play the instrument ● has control over their movements when playing ● can play as part of a group at appropriate times ● can pick out a tune on an instrument
Keeping the beat using untuned percussion instruments	● erratic ● lack of coordination ● lack of muscle control ● lack of awareness of others participating	● keeps regular beat ● strong control of movements ● can vary pace ● can tap back simple rhythms ● can make up simple rhythms
Dynamic, e.g. high/low; fast/slow; loud/soft	● cannot differentiate sounds ● cannot select appropriate dynamic for a situation, e.g. quiet for sleeping	● can differentiate sounds ● can select appropriate dynamic for a situation, e.g. loud for a storm

● Music appreciation

Children hear music all the time but this should not be equated with listening to music. Listening to pre-recorded music has an important role to play in children's musical development. While it can never replace listening to 'live music', it can nevertheless be used to create an atmosphere where children are encouraged to respond to what they hear.

Resources: CDs, tapes, DVDs, sound tracks

Activity/resources	Responses	Advanced responses
Listening to a piece of music e.g. *Peter and the Wolf*, Debussy	• no facial response to the music • no body response to the music • no awareness that music can communicate feelings • no recognition of having previously heard the music • not interested in listening to new pieces of music	• offers an emotional response • sways in time to the music • recognises the music, e.g. 'that sounds like...' • can equate a time/place/ event with the music • can re-create the music, e.g. through singing later • asks to hear favourite pieces of music • asks to hear new pieces of music

LANGUAGE

Why language?

- Language allows us to express feelings and thoughts.

- Language allows us to communicate with one another.

- Language allows us to think in the abstract.

Perhaps at the core of language is an ability to communicate – our thoughts, feelings and opinions. Human beings of course start to communicate from the minute they are born. Facial gestures and non-verbal communication lay the early building blocks for later communication through speech. A child's first words help us to see how the child is making sense of his/her world. Quickly he/she learns to combine words and begins to understand the power of language. Language also allows us to think in the abstract and to muse over complex ideas. Many parents of children who are gifted and talented in language report that their children began talking earlier than expected. These children also show a keen interest in letters and written language sooner than their chronological age would suggest. Early years educators need to offer rich language opportunities for all children.

Let's think about the activities we offer in our early years setting. We will consider what we might see children doing during certain activities and we will also consider what children, already proficient in particular skills will be doing. We will look at four common activities and their related resources in an early years setting:

Talking

Children are born communicating and their experiences thus far will have shaped and determined how articulate they have become. Certainly many young children can talk a great deal, although not all of it is meaningful to the adult. There are many occasions in the early years setting that lend themselves to the development of this skill. It is the job of the early years educator to support and develop talk through everyday interaction with the children so that all can participate in this fundamental life skill.

Resources: Books, pictures, games, artwork, circle time, snack time

Activity/resources	Responses	Advanced responses
Retelling a story	<ul><li>recounts the story out of sequence</li><li>repeats parts of the story</li><li>gives facts about the characters</li><li>unlikely to predict the outcome</li><li>factual talk</li></ul>	<ul><li>recounts story sequentially</li><li>recounts the story with accurate details</li><li>'reads between the lines'</li><li>predicts the outcome from the clues so far</li><li>uses adjectives</li><li>can create an atmosphere</li></ul>
Recounting an experience	<ul><li>get muddled up with sequence of events</li><li>become frustrated and start to repeat themselves</li><li>be concerned only with themselves</li></ul>	<ul><li>recounts events precisely</li><li>uses expression to make a point</li><li>will talk about others as well as themselves</li></ul>
Communicating with peers	<ul><li>no initiation of conversation</li><li>talks in parallel with peers</li><li>changes the topic</li></ul>	<ul><li>initiates conversation</li><li>interacts and engages in the conversation</li><li>elaborates on the topic</li></ul>
Explaining something, e.g. their art work	<ul><li>factual talk</li><li>repeats what they have heard others say</li><li>cannot give reason for personal response</li></ul>	<ul><li>uses adjectives</li><li>gives reasons for their response</li><li>can give a personal reason for their response</li></ul>

🔵 Listening/watching

Listening and watching are skills that need to be practised and honed. Indeed, there are some adults who struggle to truly listen to what is being said or see what is happening around them. However, if we are to come to some kind of understanding with our fellow human beings then listening to what they have to say is vital. Similarly, watching, when you really absorb the details of things, takes time and practice too. Helping young children to develop these skills will pay dividends in the future.

Resources: Story tapes, books, songs

Activity/resources	Responses	Advanced responses
Listening to instructions	● does not focus on what is being said ● cannot repeat back instructions ● cannot remember sequence of instructions	● listens intently ● can repeat back instructions ● can remember a number of sequential instructions
Listening to stories	● looks round the room ● asks apparent unrelated questions ● engages in some other activity e.g. rolling up a bit of paper ● talks to their peers	● listens intently ● can answer questions about the story ● can ask questions about the story ● focuses on the task ● becomes oblivious to everything round about
Listening to peers	● replies with an unrelated answer to a question ● are not aware someone is speaking to them	● answers questions being asked ● looks at their peers when they are talking
Watching	● lacks awareness ● asks lower-order questions about pictures, e.g. 'Why is the boy crying in the picture?'	● looks for detail ● asks higher-order questions, e.g. 'Why have the other children upset the boy in the picture?'

🔵 Writing

It would appear that humans have always sought to 'make a mark', for example through cave paintings and hieroglyphics. These 'marks' record for us 'life at the time'. In the 21st century our communication system relies heavily on the written as well as the spoken word, not to mention electronic communication.

From an early age most children become aware of the written word. They constantly see environmental print (e.g. road signs, shop names, the big 'M' for McDonalds). They may also see their parents, educators, siblings or relatives writing things down; for example, shopping lists, phone numbers, letters, reminders. Young children often try to copy adults and can be found 'making marks' on paper.

Often they can tell you exactly what these marks say. Children are already starting to make the connection between the written word and the conveying of meaning.

Resources: Paper, crayons, pencils, pens, chalk, chalkboards

Activity/resources	Responses	Advanced responses
Imaginative play, e.g. in the cafe/shop; travel agents; vets; hospital; etc.	● enjoys scribbling but does not connect this to real-life situations ● does not select an activity involving mark-making	● connects the marks they make with real-life situations ● actively seeks out opportunities to 'practise' writing
'Have a go' writing table	● has to be encouraged to chose the activity ● shows little interest in writing materials ● shows little interest in communicating meaning through the written word ● grasps the writing implement incorrectly	● enjoys making marks – real or pretend ● can tell you what the 'writing' says ● has a go at producing actual letters and numbers ● grips the writing implement correctly ● understands that groups of letters have meaning ● asks 'how do you write…?'
Tracing	● cannot follow the lines ● does not approach the task in a logical manner	● stays on the lines ● selects an appropriate starting point and completes the task systematically
Following patterns	● lack of hand–eye coordination ● does not start at the beginning of the pattern	● good hand–eye coordination ● starts at the beginning and progresses logically

Reading

Undoubtedly there are some young children who quickly master the art of reading and arrive in the early years setting as competent readers. However, this decoding of print is only one aspect of reading. While this ability has to be challenged and developed, there are other aspects that are equally important:

● a love of books

● the pleasure that can be gained from reading

● the opportunity to 'hear' stories

● an understanding of their cultural past through nursery rhymes, fairy tales, etc.

● comprehension

● expression and intonation.

Reading, like the other activities identified, has to be seen in the wider context of literacy so that young children become confident communicators of thoughts and feelings as well as the mechanical process of 'reading'.

Resources: Books – fiction and non-fiction, leaflets, environmental print, e.g. notices, labels, computer

Activity/resources	Responses	Advanced responses
In the library corner	• seldom chooses to visit the library corner • flits from one book to the next without looking at them • fidgets and can't sit still during library time • does not participate in activity	• can be regularly found in the library corner • selects a book and gives reasons for doing so, e.g. 'I like the cover; I've read about this character before' • selects a book and studies it in detail • listens and engages in the activity
Retelling a story using a book	• retells story out of sequence • does not link up their story with the pictures on the page • turns pages apparently on a whim	• can retell story accurately • can retell the story using phrases from the book • turns pages at appropriate point • can read 'between the lines'
Handling a book	• holds the book upside-down • reads from back to front (although this is appropriate in some cultures) • does not follow text from right to left (also appropriate in some cultures) • struggles to turn pages • 'abuses' books, e.g. throws them, scrunches up pages, etc.	• knows how to hold a book • knows about technical details, e.g. cover, title, author, etc. • knows where the story starts • knows how to turn pages • can follow text from right to left • looks after books
Environmental print	• is unaware of environmental print • does not connect notices with particular behaviour, e.g. 'only 4 at the sand'	• asks what notices round the room say • attempts to 'read' the notices using clues to predict text • keen that notices round the room should be obeyed, e.g. 'only 4 at the sand'

MATHEMATICS

Why mathematics?

- Mathematics is all around us and is an important part of everyday life.

- Mathematics can be creative and enjoyable.

- Mathematics can help us solve problems.

- There's a concern in the UK that children are not doing well at mathematics compared with other countries.

Perhaps mathematics more than any other subject is one people love to hate. Certainly large numbers of the population claim 'not to be good at mathematics'. This inability to 'do maths' is blamed on anything from poor teaching to fathers – 'my dad wasn't any good at maths either'. Somehow this is meant to make not being good at maths 'alright'. Often when considering mathematics we focus on one very narrow aspect – computation – in other words adding, subtracting, multiplying and dividing. Older children report that they do not like maths because it does not offer opportunities for creativity. And yet talk to anyone with a love of mathematics and they will tell you that maths is extremely creative. As educators we need to help children discover the joy of mathematics.

Let's think about the mathematical activities we offer in our early years setting. We will consider what we might see children doing during certain activities and we will also consider what children, already proficient in particular skills will be doing. We will look at four common activities and their related resources in an early years setting:

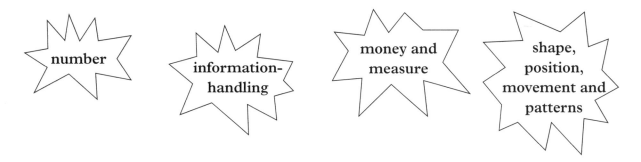

Number

Numbers are all around us in the early years setting, at home and in the community. Often activities in the early years setting do not relate directly to number but offer opportunities for young children to explore the nature and language of number. Placing the learning in a real-life context helps the child to see mathematics as a relevant aspect of life.

Resources: Cubes, beads, bricks, pictures, big books, the cafe, the shop

Activity/resources	Responses	Advanced responses
Recognising numerals, e.g. in pictures, imaginative play, etc.	• recognises significant numbers, e.g. age, house number • uses number names up to 10	• recognises a range of numbers in various contexts • uses number names beyond 10 • responds to the mathematical thinking of others
Counting, e.g. number of currants on buns	• miscounts/counts some buns twice • cannot count up to 10 consistently	• counts accurately • counts reliably up to 10 and beyond
Talking about adding on, taking away	• grasps the concept of one more/one less • grasps the concept of one more/one less but is reliant on concrete materials	• understands the concept of adding and subtracting • understands the concept of addition/subtraction in the abstract • can apply the concept within everyday situations, e.g. how many more cups do we need for snack time if there are 9 people in our group? • recognises the symbols for adding and subtracting

Shape, position, movement and patterns

Much of mathematics relates to patterns and how these relate to each other. Often in the early years setting this is restricted to recognising and re-creating patterns. We can help children to see patterns, to enjoy looking for them and to explore the relationships between shape, position, movement and number. The starting point for this should be an area of interest to the child, not some abstract task perhaps involving beads and string. Helping children to capture the enjoyment of mathematics must be key in what we do.

Resources: Jigsaws, puzzles

Activity/resources	Responses	Advanced responses
Jigsaws, puzzles	● does not turn pieces round when a piece won't fit ● does not recognise the shape/colour of the piece is the same as the shape/colour of the space ● does not see the 'big picture' ● does not approach the task in a logical manner ● becomes frustrated and gives up easily	● manipulates jigsaw pieces ● can connect shape/colour of piece to shape/colour of space ● knows what the final picture will be like ● approaches the task logically, e.g. completes the corners first ● connects the pieces with speed and ease
Positional language	● gets language of position muddled ● cannot place objects in correct position	● uses language of position accurately ● can follow instructions involving language of position ● can give instructions using positional language
Identifying shapes	● gets names of 2D and 3D shapes muddled	● can name 2D and 3D shapes accurately ● makes reference to properties of 2D and 3D shapes
Patterns and sequences	● inconsistent completion of patterns, e.g. copying Compare Bear sequence on a work card ● misrepresentation of patterns ● inability to recognise a pattern exists, e.g. becomes apparent through discussion	● copies patterns accurately ● continues patterns ● orally describes patterns

Information-handling

Making sense of the information round about us is a key skill. Learning to handle the information we gather is important if it is going to influence future decisions we make. Offering opportunities to record and interpret data is important. Supporting these skills in the early years is vital if we are to lay the foundations for future work.

Resources: Matrices, tree diagrams, the cafe

Activity/resources	Responses	Advanced responses
Sorting	• selects the most obvious way to sort • cannot articulate why they have selected that method • can only think of one way of sorting	• looks for imaginative ways of completing the task • offers more than one solution • offers more than one criterion for selection
Matrices and tree diagrams	• can sort on a matrix using one criterion • makes very little attempt to record, e.g. orders in the cafe	• can sort on a matrix using two or more criteria • able to identify own criteria for sorting • will record orders accurately in the cafe using own notation or making use of prepared charts or grids

Money and measure

In our modern world, many children never have the opportunity to handle money or to see money exchange hands. The following factors seem to have led to this situation:

- the use of credit and debit cards

- the demise of corner shops coupled with parents' fears about letting their children 'go to the shop'

- supermarkets where everything can be bought under one roof

- in schools, the rise of swipe-card cafeterias

- costs of items are beyond children's knowledge and experience of number (i.e. their number knowledge is 'up to 10' and most items cost more than this).

It is important therefore to offer opportunities within the early years setting for children to experience handling money.

Relating mathematical concepts to real life is crucial if children are going to see the relevance and meaning of activities to life outside of education. Perhaps the most common mathematical activities we engage in outside of educational institutions are measuring and weighing.

Resources: The cafe, the shop, coins, songs, rhymes, rods, rulers, height charts

Activity/resources	Responses	Advanced responses
Handling money in the shop/cafe	● little concept of the value of different coins ● little concept of different coins	● understands coins have different value ● can identify different coins
Non-standard units of measurement	● has not grasped the importance of accuracy ● will estimate but the estimate resembles a 'wild guess' ● uses the language of measure in a limited way	● measures accurately ● has grasped the importance of measuring accurately ● is willing to estimate ● estimates are reasonably accurate ● has an understanding of the comparative nature of measure ● uses the language of measure appropriately

The challenge now for the educator is how to take forward the learning of these individuals, ensuring that the 'whole child' is offered a chance to grow and develop. One common response to this challenge is to buy new resources. While new resources can be useful, in fact using the existing resources differently is often all that is required.

 SUMMING UP

Some key points have been made in this chapter in relation to gifted and talented children's responses to resources and activities.

- The cross-curricular nature of problem-solving.

- The common resources and activities on offer across four specific curricular areas.

- The skills and abilities children and gifted and talented children might be presenting in each of the curricular areas when using these resources and engaging in the activities.

Chapter 4

Physical movement/motor development

This chapter will:

- consider why it is important to develop and challenge the skills young children display in physical movement/motor development.

- suggest a planning framework for activities.

- offer some activities to challenge young children in their learning.

As suggested in Chapter 3, many young children will already have well-developed skills in this area and so the early years educator needs to consider how they will develop and challenge these skills in an inclusive framework. Each child has a right to a challenging learning experience, and the area of physical movement and motor development is no exception.

However, we need to guard against identifying and hot-housing young children who show particular ability. The Scottish Sport's Council recently said that early identification is not always a good thing. Indeed, it can lead to children reaching a plateau and may in fact hinder them from becoming sportsmen and women in the future. Young muscles and skeletons have to be allowed to form and develop without being damaged. Getting the balance between early identification and appropriate challenge at the right level is not easy. Perhaps it brings us once again to the notion that in early years we should be focusing on offering challenging opportunities and next steps. While the temptation for educators may be to introduce structured games and activities, we should instead be helping young children first and foremost to enjoy movement.

- Develop existing skills.

- Help children to transfer skills they already possess from one situation to another.

- Offer new physical movement and motor development opportunities.

- Help children of all abilities to work together.

- Help children to enjoy moving.

So where do we start?

One of the first things to do, regardless of what skill you are wanting to challenge, is to plan the activity. Planning an activity allows you to think about where the children are in their learning and how you would like to move their learning forward. It also offers you an opportunity to talk with the children and find out what they're interested in and how they like to learn. For example, some children will be:

- *active* learners – they like to learn by doing.

- *visual* learners – they like to learn by watching.

- *participative* learners – they like to learn by copying a more knowledgeable other.

Knowing about how the child likes to learn will help you to plan more appropriate learning tasks.

While the focus here is on young children who are already displaying some degree of ability, this outline can be used for planning the learning of any child. Planning requires the following to be considered:

- What can the child already do?

- Is the child working independently on the skill?

- Are the present activities too easy for the child?

- What is the child interested in?

- Where do I want to take their learning next?

- What is the best way to help them get there?

- Implications for organisation.

A planning framework sheet where you can jot down some answers to these questions will allow you to think about how you will challenge a child's learning. You can also add these to the child's folio. Over time this will result in a developmental picture of the planning that has taken place for that child.

Planning framework

With the points for good practice and the planning framework in mind, the rest of this chapter suggests activities that will allow you to challenge young children and take forward their learning.
They have been developed with the busy educator in mind. They offer ready-to-use activities that can be adapted to suit the needs of individual early years settings.

Photocopy these pages and keep them in a ring binder. You can add to them as you develop activities yourself. If you keep them in a central place, everyone can access them. This will allow your early years setting to build up a bank of challenging activities.

Question	Comment
What can the child already do?	
Is the child working independently?	
In what ways are the present activities too easy for the child?	
What do I want the child to learn? Relate to Learning Outcomes/Desirable Outcomes	
What is the best way to help them to learn?	
Implications for organisation	

CHALLENGING ACTIVITIES

1. Climbing

Resource: Climbing apparatus

Activity/resources	Advanced responses	Possible challenging activities
Climbing, e.g. on apparatus	• have confidence on apparatus • hold body weight with ease • display effortless, flowing movements as they climb • use opposite arm/leg action • have a strong grasp of the bars	1 climb vertically using different parts of the body differently or climb horizontally using different parts of the body differently 2 create a problem-solving type activity

1. An adult should supervise these activities. Start by explaining what the words 'vertical' and 'horizontal' mean. Ask the children if they can think of animals that move horizontally and vertically. They might, for example, suggest a snake and a chimpanzee. Have a collection of pictures ready for the children to look at and identify whether they show people, animals or objects moving vertically or horizontally. Ask the children to climb up the climbing frame but suggest that they can only use certain parts of their body. For example, they could use:

    ● hands only

    ● right hand and left leg only

    ● left hand and right leg only

    ● different kinds of grips.

2. Link the work you do at the climbing frame to your topic work. For example, if you are learning about the sea you could:

    ● Put a piece of blue material under the climbing frame.

    ● Explain to the children that the climbing frame is a desert island and they are stranded on the island.

    ● Tell them that if they can reach the top of the island they will find food and water and they will be able to wave for help.

    ● Tell them they can climb around the apparatus, over the apparatus and along the apparatus but that they must not fall off because sharks swim in the sea around the island (alternatively, tell them they can only climb around the apparatus, they are not allowed to go over it, along it or through it).

● You could add a further challenge by linking up two children with a short length of rope, like mountain climbers, and ask them to reach the top of the island together. **This activity would need close adult supervision.**

This kind of work on the climbing frame can be carried over to art and design work, for example, where the children might paint or make a model of their escape from the island.

2. Running

Resource: Large spaces

Activity/resources	Advanced responses	Possible challenging activities
Running	● bent forwards ● flowing action ● leg and arm movements in opposition to each other ● head up ● during the running process the runner is in the air ● the supporting leg is firm and extended	1 explore changes of direction 2 consider different kinds of running 3 run in different paths 4 run in relation to obstacles or people

1. Children need to explore how their running changes according to the amount of space they have. They also need to be aware of direction as they run. Even children who have a strong running action need to know how to harness this ability and use it to their advantage. Ask the children to run in different directions:

● forwards

● backwards

● sideways

● in circles.

Change the space you offer the children. You could have:

● a large space

● a small space

● an unusually shaped space

● a large space with obstacles in it

● a small space with obstacles in it

● an unusually shaped space with obstacles in it.

2. Children also need to be aware of different types of running. Ask them to:

    - run like an angry wild animal

    - run like a balloon floating in the air

    - run a short distance very quickly

    - run a longer distance at a slower pace.

3. Having explored changes of direction, space and different kinds of running, children now need to be able to run in specific pathways. You could:

    - set out skittles and ask the children to run between them

    - lay out hoops and ask the children to run from the red one to blue one, etc.

    - ask the children to run round the room visiting particular corners or features in a particular order.

    - ask the children to make up their own path for running.

    - have the children make up pathways for others.

4. Learning to run in relation to obstacles or people will be an important skill for later when games skills are introduced. Learning the basics of these skills in a non-competitive setting and in relation to activities above will support children in their development and learning. You could:

    - ask the children to sidestep each other as they run round the room

    - roll a large ball across the room and ask the children to sidestep it

    - ask the children to run in pairs with one chasing the other; they have to sidestep each other as they run

    - ask the children to keep running at the same pace as they sidestep an object or a person.

3. Throwing

Resources: Large balls, beanbags, small balls, quoits

Activity/resources	Advanced responses	Possible challenging activities
Throwing, e.g. overarm throw	• arm swings back prior to throw • weight transfers forwards • non-throwing arm is held out to aid balance • steps forward on opposite foot to throwing arm • throwing arm follows through towards the direction of the throw	1 use a variety of objects when throwing 2 throwing for distance 3 throwing for accuracy 4 have the child be aware of body movements as they throw

1. Children should be exposed to a variety of appropriate objects for throwing. A useful discussion can ensue as to what is or is not appropriate. Common objects to be found in an early years setting include:

   - balls of various sizes and made from various materials
   - quoits
   - foam javelins
   - beanbags
   - frisbees
   - foam darts.

2. Discuss with the children the idea of throwing something a distance. Children can suggest a time when throwing something a distance would be useful. Pictures of people throwing things, e.g. javelin throwing, shot put, etc. can be cut out of magazines or newspapers or found on the Internet. More unusual throwing events can be displayed and discussed, e.g. welly-throwing or tossing the caber at a Highland Games. Allow the children opportunity to experiment with throwing objects a distance. Children can find out the shape of object that is easier to throw or travels furthest. Children should be encouraged to try out a range of throws:

   - underarm
   - overarm
   - sideways.

   They should also be encouraged to throw objects different distances, increasing in length as the child progresses. They should also become aware of what kind of throw is best for the task. For example, which kind of throw is best if we want to:

   - throw for speed
   - throw for accuracy
   - throw to let someone hit it with a bat
   - throw to hit a target?

3. Accurate throwing is important, for safety among other things. Offering children the opportunity to throw for accuracy will help them to develop their already evident abilities and skills. You should:

   - set up a target for the children to aim for or let the children select a target
   - increase the distance between the child and the target
   - increase or decrease the height of the target
   - ask the child to stand inside a hoop when they throw
   - make the target a moving target

- use a variety of objects to hit the target

- add challenges, e.g. can they hit the target if they close one eye, are blindfolded, stand with their back to the target, throw the object between their legs?

4. Children with ability will often almost naturally move their bodies in a particular way when throwing. Pointing out why they are throwing with accuracy can be helpful when the child starts to refine these movements even further.

- Talk with the child about the position their body is in as they throw.

- Encourage the child to change their body positions.

- Ask the child to explain why the object hits the target when they stand a particular way.

4. Jumping

Resource: Flat space

Activity/resources	Advanced responses	Challenging activities
Jumping, e.g. a vertical jump	• squat down prior to jumping • legs extend and stretch • body is fully stretched when in the air • controlled landing with knees and ankles bent	1 explore different kinds of landing 2 jump for height 3 jump for distance 4 combine activities 5 problem-solving activities

1. Jumping should only take place on soft surfaces such as mats or grass. Landing after a jump is an important part of the jump itself. Once the child can land comfortably on two feet, they should be asked to:

- land on one foot

- land crouched down

- land on two feet in a balanced position

- land on one foot in a balanced position.

2. Children should be encouraged to jump for height. This is another skill that can be developed once the child is older and participating in structured games, e.g. netball, volleyball. Children should be asked to:

- burst into the air from a crouched position

- explode into the air and land in a different place from the starting position

- use their arms to propel them into the air

- experiment taking off and landing on one foot and two feet and deciding which one thrusts them higher into the air.

3.   As well as propelling themselves into the air when jumping, jumping for distance can also be developed. Ask the children to:

- take off from two feet and land further forward on one foot

- take off from one foot and land further forward on two feet

- jump and land in a diagonal position from where they started

- jump as far as they can.

4.   Combining activities and movements offers children the opportunity to use their imaginations and to think creatively. Explain that children can combine any of the jumping movements they can do to make a sequence. Children could:

- jump, turn round in the air and land

- combine two kinds of jumps, e.g. one jump for height and one for distance

- jump off a piece of apparatus, e.g. a bench, and see how far they can go before landing

- hop a distance then jump for height.

5.   As with the climbing frame, it's probably best to integrate this kind of activity with your topic work. For example, if you were learning about the jungle:

- Each child selects an animal they have been learning about.

- Hoops can be laid out on the floor.

- Each hoop represents a tree top.

- A bench can be set out to represent the animal's den.

- Children have to reach their den by jumping into each of the hoops.

- The hoops can be laid out in varying measures apart.

- Children should be encouraged to explore using a range of jumps. This would include experimenting with take-offs and landings.

- To add extra challenge the children could pick up items from each hoop that have to be delivered safely to the den. You could use beanbags, foam balls, etc., as the objects to be collected.

5. Using a bat and ball

Resources: Various size balls, various size bats

Activity/resources	Advanced responses	Challenging activities
Using a bat and ball	• bat is in position to receive the ball • body faces the side in preparation • weight is moved to front foot • eyes follow the ball through the air • bat hits ball with sweeping action	1 use varying size of equipment 2 hit the ball in a variety of ways 3 vary the trajectory of the ball 4 use the bat to direct the ball through obstacles

1. Using varying of size of equipment will help the child to refine and hone their skills and abilities. You can use:

    - large balls, small bat

    - small balls, large bat

    - a cricket bat

    - a baseball bat

    - a tennis racquet

    - a table-tennis bat

    - footballs

    - foam balls

    - tennis balls

    - plastic lightweight balls.

    Children can be encouraged to explore the differences that the different types of bats and balls make.

2. When children are hitting accurately, they can be challenged by asking them to:

    - tap the ball gently

    - hit the ball hard

    - hit the ball in a particular direction

    - hit the ball so that it lands and bounces in a hoop.

3. Tying in with point 2 above, children can be asked to:

    ● hit the ball so that it makes a large arc in the sky

    ● hit the ball so that it skims across the floor

    ● hit the ball so that it goes in a straight line from the bat

    ● hit the ball so that it arcs before it bounces.

4. Being able to hit the ball with some degree of accuracy is a skill that will be beneficial as structured games are played later on. Experimenting with a bat, ball and objects at this stage will allow the children to:

    ● develop hand–eye coordination

    ● estimate distance and speed

    ● understand the need for accuracy when hitting the ball.

    The room can be set up with different obstacles laid out. For example:

    ● rows of skittles could be placed in a twisting pathway

    ● skittles and canes can be set up in a pathway.

● An extra activity

If your early years setting has access to the school gym hall, arrange to meet with an older class. Organise the children into groups so that an older child and a younger child are working together. The older child can act as a 'buddy' to the younger child. Together they can explore:

● ways of travelling across the floor or equipment together

● ways of rolling across mats

● bat-and-ball activities

● running activities.

As well as having an impact on physical movement, the teaming up of younger children with older children also allows friendships to develop and often these friendships are carried on into the playground or school yard where incidents of bullying can be lessened as children learn to communicate with one another and care for one another.

Many of these activities are adult-led. For an even richer learning experience ask the children to help you devise these.

SUMMING UP

Some key points and suggestions have been made in this chapter in relation to challenging activities in the area of physical and motor development. They include:

- the importance of developing and challenging the skills young children display in physical movement/motor development
- a planning framework for activities
- some activities to challenge young children in their learning.

Chapter 5

Music

This chapter will:

- consider why it is important to develop and challenge the skills young children display in music.

- suggest a planning framework for activities.

- offer some activities to challenge young children in their learning.

There is no doubt that child prodigies exist. However, to suggest that musical ability only lies within a few would not give us a true picture of the breadth of musical talent that exists in our early years settings. Unquestionably some children arrive at our early years setting displaying signs of early ability in music and these children and their abilities must be challenged and developed. Nonetheless, one of the fundamental arguments in this book is that children need to develop in a rounded way and so to focus purely on the development of their musical abilities at the expense of others may well be detrimental to their overall development.

So where do we start?

One of the first things to do, regardless of what skill you are wanting to challenge, is to plan the activity. Planning an activity allows you to think about where the children are in their learning and how you would like to move their learning forward. It also offers you an opportunity to talk with the children and find out what they're interested in and how they like to learn. For example, some children will be:

- *active learners* – they like to learn by doing.

- *visual learners* – they like to learn by watching.

- *participative learners* – they like to learn by copying a more knowledge-able other.

- Develop existing skills.

- Help children to transfer skills they already possess from one situation to another.

- Offer new music opportunities.

- Help children of all abilities to work together.

- Help children to enjoy music.

Knowing about how the child likes to learn will help you to plan more appropriate learning tasks. Planning requires the following to be considered:

- What can the child already do?

- Is the child working independently on the skill?

- Are the present activities too easy for the child?

- What is the child interested in?

- Where do I want to take their learning next?

- What is the best way to help them get there?

- Implications for organisation.

A planning framework sheet where you can jot down some answers to these questions will allow you to think about how you will challenge a child's learning. You can also add these to the child's folio. Over time this will result in a developmental picture of the planning that has taken place for that child. With the points for good practice and the planning framework in mind, the rest of this chapter suggests activities that will allow you to challenge young children and take forward their learning. They have been developed with the busy educator in mind. They offer ready-to-use activities that can be adapted to suit the needs of individual early years settings.

Planning framework

Photocopy these pages and keep them in a ring binder. You can add to them as you develop activities yourself. If you keep them in a central place, everyone can access them. This will allow your early years setting to build up a bank of challenging activities.

Question	Comment
What can the child already do?	
Is the child working independently?	
In what ways are the present activities too easy for the child?	
What do I want the child to learn? Relate to Learning Outcomes/Desirable Outcomes	
What is the best way to help them to learn?	
Implications for organisation	

CHALLENGING ACTIVITIES

1. Singing

Resources: Nursery rhymes, action songs, counting songs, echo songs, tapes, CDs

Activity/resources	Advanced responses	Possible challenging activities
Singing a song. 'Okki Tokki Unga': Action Songs for Children; Apusskidu: Songs for Children; Mango Spice: 44 Caribbean Songs; Tongo: Count Me In: 44 Songs and Rhymes about Numbers; Tom Thumb's Musical Maths: Developing Maths Skills with Simple Songs; etc.	● enthusiastic ● responds to activities ● can hold a tune ● makes up songs ● enjoys performing ● recognises familiar songs in varying contexts, e.g. on TV	1 offer opportunities for informal singing 2 make a book about their favourite songs 3 ask the child to teach the group/adults a song 4 develop actions for songs 5 begin using invented notation 6 start singing two- and three-part songs

1. As children move around the early years setting, encourage them to take part in spontaneous singing. This can happen in any area of the early years setting and can happen indoors or out of doors or when engaging in another task. This is important for building up creativity in music. If the singing occurs outdoors, it is a good place to explore dynamics – How loud can you sing? How softly can you sing? Children can also be asked to sing their song in a particular style:

    ● Country and Western style

    ● opera style

    ● jazz style

    ● boy-band style

    ● lullaby style.

2. Ask children to talk about their favourite songs. Ask them to produce pictures about their song to make into a book for others to use. Have the children illustrate the book. This offers opportunity for developing language – written, musical and spoken. This encourages children to:

    ● think about the words they are singing

    ● think about the meaning the song conveys

    ● use music as a stimulus for creative art work.

3. If children are holding a tune well of a song they know, and if they have confidence, ask them to teach the group and/or the adults the song. This offers wonderful opportunities for the children to:

- engage in leader–chorus activities where the child is the leader

- feel that their musical knowledge is respected and valued

- listen to the sounds being produced by themselves and others.

4. If the children can sing a song unfamiliar to the early years setting, actions can be devised to go with the song by:

- the children themselves

- the adult

- the other children in the group

- acting out the meaning of the words

- listening to the pattern of the tune, e.g. when the tune 'goes up'/'gets higher', the action 'goes up'/'gets higher', etc.

5. The adult can work with the child in creating a written response in the form of invented notations for the song they are singing. 'Notation' is the name given to pictorial representations that will help children to develop an awareness of musical structures and conventions. These invented notations might include:

- lines

- curls

- squiggles

- a combination of symbols and pictures.

6. When the child is sustaining a tune, then two- and three-part songs and rounds can be introduced. This allows the child to:

- be part of a collective singing group

- begin to hear and identify harmonies.

● 2. Instruments and sound-making

Resources: Tuned percussion instruments, e.g. chime bars, hand chimes, piano; untuned percussion, e.g. drums, woodblocks, bells, shakers, triangles, cymbals, tambourines

Activity/resources	Advanced responses	Challenging activities
Instruments and sound-making	● remembers how to hold and play the instrument ● has control over their movements when playing ● can play as part of a group at appropriate times ● can pick out a tune on an instrument	1 develop a musical 'conversation' between the adult and the child or between children 2 encourage children to play instruments in response to other children's movements 3 encourage children to play instruments for other children to respond to in their movements
Keeping the beat using untuned percussion instruments	● keeps regular beat ● strong control of movements ● can vary pace ● can tap back simple rhythms ● can make up simple rhythms	4 record the child playing instruments 5 start to make connections between sounds and mark-making, e.g. follow simple pictorial notation
Dynamics, e.g. high/low; fast/slow; loud/soft	● can differentiate sounds ● can select appropriate dynamic for a situation, e.g. loud for a storm	6 string together sounds to create a story or sound picture

1. Developing musical 'conversations' can involve the adult in music-making alongside the child or the child in music-making alongside a peer or older child. In each case the lead comes from the child. This kind of musical conversation includes:

    ● using tuned percussion instruments to mimic the child

    ● using untuned percussion instruments to mimic the child

    ● using parts of the body, e.g. shoulders, knees, elbows, to respond to the child's rhythm

    ● allowing the child to play the rhythm and the partner playing it back.

2. As their peers are moving about the early years setting or are in the gym, the child can respond to this movement by:

    ● selecting and playing an appropriate instrument to accompany the movement

- asking the children to move according to the type of instrument selected, e.g. bells suggest light movements, two-tone wood block suggests hopping, stilted movements

- using instruments and voice to accompany the children's movement.

3. Have the child select a range of instruments. As they play the instruments, have their peers move around the early years setting or gym in a way that reflects the sounds they hear. This could be connected to topic work; for example, if discussing the weather, the child could select instruments that reflect a storm, a sunny day, a cold day, etc.

4. A tape recorder can be set up in the music corner to record the children as they play. This allows the children and the adults to:

- hear the sound they produce

- accompany themselves on the tape, thus multi-layering the sounds they create

- discuss the sounds created

- return to the music at a later date

- use the created music as a stimulus for art work, creative writing, exploring nature, devising a sound picture.

5. A range of instruments – tuned, untuned and homemade – should be available and children should be encouraged to explore the sounds these make. Discussing with the child the shape of the sounds, words that describe the sounds and what the sound sounds like will help them to:

- begin to visualise a written mark that corresponds to the sound

- experiment with shapes on paper and sounds produced

- read the marks and be able to reproduce a sound at a later date.

6. Using a selection of instruments (as described in point 5 above), children can create sounds to accompany a story. This story can be a well-known tale or one that the children have written themselves. Building on experimenting with sounds, the children can start to create moods by:

- selecting an appropriate instrument to create the effect they desire

- alter the response to the story by playing softly, loudly etc

- alter the response by changing the tone, e.g. use a different beater

- begin to associate music with feelings and moods and recognising that these can alter.

3. Music appreciation

Resources: CDs, tapes, DVDs, sound tracks

Activity/resources	Advanced responses	Challenging activities
Listening to a piece of music, e.g. Peter and the Wolf, Debussy	• offers an emotional response • sways in time to the music • recognises the music, e.g. 'that sounds like...' • can equate a time/place/event with the music • can re-create the music, e.g. through singing later • asks to hear favourite pieces of music • asks to hear new pieces of music	1 offer a range of listening material 2 provide an area with instruments, ribbons and other props for responding to music 3 link listening to music to other curricular areas, e.g. art, story corner 4 take time to talk to the child about their music preferences 5 use spoken language to respond to music 6 create an environmental map of sound 7 invite musicians – professional, parents, older children – to play for the children

1. It is important that children have the opportunity to hear a range of music. A music library should be built up and should include a variety of types of music. Children can be encouraged to bring in their favourite CDs from home. The variety should include:

- jazz

- rhythm and blues

- rap

- opera

- Country and Western

- orchestral

- electronically produced music

- steel band

- African drumming music

- house music

- string quartet

- choir music.

2. Alongside the listening corner should be an area that allows children to respond in a physical and concrete way to the music they are hearing. Instruments, ribbons, paper and crayons, scarves, strips of material can be available. Children should be encouraged to:

   - explore ways of using the props to demonstrate their understanding of the music

   - select the appropriate prop for the kind of music being played, e.g. a ribbon floating to denote light, airy music

   - colour or draw what the music is suggesting to them.

3. An extension of the work suggested above is to explicitly connect the music to other curricular areas. A deliberate linking of subjects by the adult will allow children to explore:

   - the cross-curricular nature of music

   - the cross-curricular nature of learning

   - the importance of the transfer of skills from one setting to another.

4. Helping children to articulate what it is they like about particular music and why helps the children to feel valued and allows the educator to enter the world of the children as they listen to music. It is important to:

   - accept the reasons the children present for liking/disliking particular music

   - accept that musical tastes are different for different people

   - allow children to explore their feelings and fears through music

   - acknowledge that music is a very powerful and emotive tool

   - explore cultures through listening to different music.

5. Music can be used as a stimulus for language development. Listening to a variety of music will allow the educator and child to:

   - explore words to explain sounds

   - translate feelings into words

   - broaden vocabulary through music

   - investigate the relationship between words and nonsense words as the children describe what they are hearing.

6. Going for a walk around the early years setting and listening to the everyday sounds will allow you to build up an environmental 'sound map'. This encourages children to:

   - listen for detail

   - listen for natural sounds

- listen for repeated pattern sounds

- devise ways of recoding these sounds symbolically to share with others.

7. For many people nothing can compare to hearing live music. Invite professional musicians, parents who play an instrument or older children who play an instrument to your early years setting to play and talk about their instrument. This allows children to:

- hear first-hand about an instrument

- see an instrument close up

- hear the tone and volume of an instrument for themselves

- find out about different families of instruments, i.e. string, woodwind, brass, percussion

- play along on instruments with a live musician.

- sing with a live accompaniment.

An extra activity

As part of your themed work, work with the children to:

- write a story line for a play

- write a script for your story line

- compose songs for your script

- compose a sound picture to accompany your script and songs

- make instruments to use as part of the sound picture

- make costumes and masks for the play

- choreograph the play

- rehearse your work

- perform the play for older children, parents, the community.

This will challenge the child with abilities but, equally importantly, it will be good fun and a learning experience for all.

Many of these activities are adult-led. For an even richer learning experience ask the children to help you devise these.

SUMMING UP

Some key points and suggestions have been made in this chapter in relation to challenging activities in the area of music. They include:

- the importance of developing and challenging the skills young children display in music

- a planning framework for activities

- some activities to challenge young children in their learning.

Chapter 6

Language

This chapter will:

- consider why it is important to develop and challenge the skills young children display in language.

- suggest a planning framework for activities.

- offer some activities to challenge young children in their learning.

Within the early years setting, 'language' is often an umbrella term for talking, reading, writing and listening. In other words, it encompasses language and literacy. However, it is often the extremely articulate child who 'stands out' in an early years setting. They communicate in a way, on a level and use vocabulary, that their peers do not. While it is important to challenge and recognise this ability, the early years educator must be careful not to confuse precocious speech with outstanding linguistic ability. We should be aiming for a wide and rich language experience that ensures all children have the opportunity to develop and:

- play with words

- come into contact with the social nature of language

- make marks for meaning

- enter the world of print

- learn to appreciate others' viewpoints.

Developing these wide ranging language skills will help the child to develop linguistically. They will not simply become 'better readers'.

- Develop existing skills.

- Help children to transfer skills they already possess from one situation to another.

- Offer new language-rich opportunities.

- Help children of all abilities to work together.

- Help children to enjoy language.

So where do we start?

One of the first things to do, regardless of what skill you are wanting to challenge, is to plan the activity. Planning an activity allows you to think about where the children are in their learning and how you would like to move their learning forward. It also offers you an opportunity to talk with the children and find out what they're interested in and how they like to learn. For example, some children will be:

- *active* learners – they like to learn by doing.

- *visual* learners – they like to learn by watching.

- *participative* learners – they like to learn by copying a more knowledgeable other.

Knowing about how the child likes to learn will help you to plan more appropriate learning tasks. Planning requires the following to be considered:

- What can the child already do?

- Is the child working independently on the skill?

- Are the present activities too easy for the child?

- What is the child interested in?

- Where do I want to take their learning next?

- What is the best way to help them get there?

- Implications for organisation.

A planning framework sheet where you can jot down some answers to these questions will allow you to think about how you will challenge a child's learning. You can also add these to the child's folio. Over time this will result in a developmental picture of the planning that has taken place for that child.

Planning framework

With the points for good practice and the planning framework in mind, the rest of this chapter suggests activities that will allow you to challenge young children and take forward their learning. They have been developed with the busy educator in mind. They offer ready to use activities that can be adapted to suit the needs of individual early years settings.

Photocopy these pages and keep them in a ring binder. You can add to them as you develop activities yourself. If you keep them in a central place, everyone can access them. This will allow your early years setting to build up a bank of challenging activities.

Question	Comment
What can the child already do?	
Is the child working independently?	
In what ways are the present activities too easy for the child?	
What do I want the child to learn? Relate to Learning Outcomes/Desirable Outcomes	
What is the best way to help them to learn?	
Implications for organisation	

CHALLENGING ACTIVITIES

1. Talking

Resources: Books, pictures, games, artwork, circle time, snack time

Activity/resources	Advanced responses	Challenging activities
Retelling a story	● recounts story sequentially ● recounts the story with accurate details ● 'reads between the lines' ● predicts the outcome from the clues so far ● uses adjectives ● can create an atmosphere	1 develop story-telling skills 2 act out the story
Recounting an experience	● recounts events precisely ● uses expression to make a point ● will talk about others as well as themselves	3 create a narrative about themselves
Communicating with peers	● initiates conversation ● interacts and engages in the conversation ● elaborates on the topic	4 develop conversations with peers
Explaining something, e.g. their art work	● uses adjectives ● gives reasons for their response ● can give a personal reason for their response	5 talking with peers

1. Children should be encouraged to develop story-telling skills alongside retelling stories. This is quite different from telling a story through reading a book. To develop these skills they should:

    ● Be encouraged to think of a storyline beforehand: what exciting things will happen in the story; how will they communicate that to their audience; how will the story finish?

    ● Encourage the children to listen to the sounds of the words as they say them. They should include nonsense words, rhyming words, unusual words. Spoken language should be fun!

    ● Suggest that repeated phrases in a story means that their peers can join in the story-telling.

    ● Help the children to develop different voices for different characters. This will help their audience relate to the characters.

At first the stories will be quite short. This is OK. Stories will expand and develop as the story-teller becomes familiar and secure in the art of story-telling.

2. Favourite stories can be acted out with props. The props can be made by the children and/or educator or can be gathered specifically for the purpose. The acting out of the story allows the children to explore and experiment with voice production. The re-creation of well-known stories is important in the development of story structure and language. It offers opportunities to expand vocabulary and to make up fun, rhyming words.

3. While retelling a familiar story is important, it is also important to help children to develop 'personal narratives'. In other words, they should create a story about themselves. This is not a fantasy type of story but a real account of their lives. Children should be encouraged to share with others significant things that are happening in their lives. For example, if a child has a birthday they can tell their peers about the birthday celebrations; they can show how much they have grown and developed since their last birthday; they can consider how much they have changed since they were born. Significant achievements in the early years setting and beyond can be discussed so that a full biographical picture can emerge. This acknowledgement of them as a person will contribute to their identity and will help them to feel part of the learning community to which they belong.

4. Children who are highly able can often communicate extremely well with adults but struggle to communicate with their age peers. The early years setting offers wonderful opportunities for developing communication:

   Play. Carefully constructed role-play or problem-solving situations can encourage children to communicate and engage in collaborative play. When children are inclined to play alone or in parallel play (as often more able children are) then the role of the adult is crucial in ensuring that collaborative play happens. Gentle guidance and careful questioning for opinions or thoughts by the adult can become the link between the children. This helps children to consider others' opinions and feelings and can help them to begin to connect to the others around them even when they appear to think differently.

   Role-play with 'expert adults' allows us to capitalise on their ability to communicate with adults. For example, an orthopaedic nurse working in the hospital corner brought technical knowledge and vocabulary to the role-play that I was not able to provide. She also helped the children to build 'real life' junk model hospital equipment. Working with these children in the hospital corner and during the art and craft activity allowed her to discuss how equipment works, how bones are formed and how to keep bones healthy. She was also able to talk about the qualities and attributes necessary for nursing using her technical expertise and the experiences of the children in the group who had been in hospital. Working collaboratively on a task, being able to discuss technical details and to use the information other children had provided allowed the able child to be challenged appropriately but also to feel part of the group discussion.

Working together on a task. As with play, some more able children would rather work alone than with someone else. While independent working should be encouraged, children must also learn to work together. Setting a task, such as a problem-solving task, and assigning key roles and tasks within the activity will allow adults to observe the kind of interaction that takes place. Assigning of roles and tasks means that all are clear about what is expected of them. The need to collaborate to achieve the outcome will result in children having to communicate with one another. Individual strengths can be utilised here. For example, if the children were to 'build an ambulance with doors that open', a child with good organisational skills can be responsible for gathering the necessary equipment; a child with good negotiating skills can be responsible for gathering the ideas for planning the design; a child with good motor development can be responsible for cutting out or manipulating the materials; a child with good communication skills can be responsible for reporting back to the wider group. Once secure in their roles, they can be encouraged to try out different roles.

5. Being able to articulate thoughts and feelings is an important part of language development. We need to develop skills that allow us to think in difficult and abstract ways. We can do this in the following ways:

- Using 'what if' questions allows already articulate children to explore things from a different perspective.

- Brainstorm with the children to develop their ideas and the information they have acquired. What else can they find out? What are they going to do with the knowledge now? How else can they express that information and knowledge, e.g. through art, music, creative movement, drama, science experiments?

2. Listening/watching

Resources: Story tapes, books, songs

Activity/resources	Advanced responses	Challenging activities
Listening to instructions	• listens intently • can repeat back instructions • can remember a number of sequential instructions	1 increase complexity of instruction
Listening to stories	• listens intently • can answer questions about the story • can ask questions about the story • focuses on the task • becomes oblivious to everything round about	2 reading for meaning 3 'feeling' detectives
Listening to peers	• answers questions being asked • looks at their peers when they are talking	4 responding to others 5 listening in a group
Watching	• looks for detail • asks higher-order questions, e.g. why have the other children upset the boy in the picture?	6 specific observations

1. Children can be given increasingly complex instructions. Adjectives can be added and directional language can be included. For example:

    ● Go to the large red cupboard and open the door. On the second top shelf, underneath the boxes of jigsaws you will find the paintbrushes. Can you bring the paintbrushes to me?

2. Asking questions about a text allows the child to understand the text and to apportion meaning to it. More able children often have a heightened sense in relation to feelings and empathy and they often have a well-developed awareness of justice and injustice. Offering children opportunities to ask questions about stories and characters that address these important issues in life allows children to feel they have explored difficult questions in a safe and secure environment. Adults should:

    ● re-read the text so children can relate to the story

    ● create opportunities to identify favourite stories and characters

    ● create opportunities for talking

    ● not be afraid to tackle difficult life issues head-on.

3. Children can be encouraged to listen for and identify words in the story or poem that are about feelings such as:

- sad

- happy

- cry

- angry

- scream

- hug

- kiss

- smile.

Having identified them, discussion can take place about how we convey these feelings and emotions to others.

4.   Children need to learn to communicate and respond to others. Young children often find this hard and it is easier to lash out at someone than to reason and negotiate with them. The development of this area is inextricably linked with social and emotional development. Listening to others and responding appropriately takes time and practice. Children need to:

- read the child's face, i.e. read the signs. Do they look happy? Do they look angry?

- See the other child's point of view; for example, if I take the crayon it will make him unhappy.

Cards with faces on it can be made. The children can help to select faces and stick them onto cards. They can also draw faces representing various emotions. This helps the children to think about facial features – e.g. screwed-up eyes when angry, wide-open eyes when smiling, etc. This can be related to activity 3 above. Helping children to recognise emotions and to recognise that behaviour is related to emotions will help the gifted and talented child to react more appropriately. For example, we need to help children to realise that they hit the child because they were feeling angry. Connecting feelings to behaviour can be a powerful experience for the children. Articulate gifted and talented children will often understand this relationship and be able, with support, to verbalise their feelings.

5.   Group situations do not reflect the flow of natural conversations. However, group discussion times do offer an opportunity to develop turn-taking. If children are reporting back on their work, telling a story or offering a point of view, then able children can be encouraged to ask questions arising from the details being given.

6.   Observant children can be asked to look for a specific point in a picture or a story. For example:

- How does the digger get across the bridge?

- In what ways is the blue house different from the red one?

3. Writing

Resources: Paper, crayons, pencils, pens, chalk, chalkboards

Activity/resources	Advanced responses	Challenging activities
Imaginative play, e.g. in the cafe/shop; travel agents; vets; hospital; etc.	• connects the marks they make with real-life situations • actively seeks out opportunities to 'practise' writing	1 offer real-life opportunities
'Have a go' writing table	• enjoys making marks – real or pretend • can tell you what the 'writing' says • has a go at producing actual letters and numbers • grips the writing implement correctly • understands that groups of letters have meaning • asks 'how do you write...?'	2 use a variety of writing materials 3 advice and guidance on the formation of letters 4 computer work
Tracing and following patterns	• stays on the lines • selects an appropriate starting point and completes the task systematically • good hand–eye coordination • starts at the beginning and progresses logically	5 more intricate patterns 6 picture closure

1. As an extension to the child's eagerness to make meaningful marks a variety of situations can be created that incorporate the need to 'write'. For example:

   ● the cafe – orders, till receipts, menus, signs

   ● the shop – shopping lists, special offers, till receipts, credit card transactions

   ● the travel agents – details of holidays, client details

   ● the hospital – recording of temperatures, case notes, prescriptions, patients' details

   ● the vet – pet's details, case notes.

   If any parents or adults in the community can be involved in these role-play situations then they should be encouraged to work alongside the children, adding a further dimension to the 'real-life' approach. Interacting with adults in this way:

   ● allows the children to hear a wider vocabulary related to the area

   ● offers them an opportunity to see real-life examples of how to deal with and record situations

- allows adults with expert knowledge to develop the skills and abilities the child may present.

2. A variety of writing implements should be on offer to the children. Some able children do not like to work with lead pencils because of the texture and sound they make, so early years settings should ensure that they offer variety of mark-making tools, including:

- felt pens

- calligraphy pens

- brush felt pens

- large bulbous ballpoint pens

- artists' pencils

- joiners' pencils

- gel pens.

Remember that the aim here is to encourage and develop the interest in writing. The focus should be on flow and rhythmic writing style, not on spelling and letter formation.

3. When children are showing an interest in forming letters adults, can help and support them in this by:

- Introducing them to the formation of letters in, for example, their name.

- Using sand in a tray for practising letter formation. The tactile approach works well for some children and a shake of the tray means mistakes are easily wiped out.

- Making sandpaper letters to promote letter formation as children can 'feel' the shape of a letter. Doing this with their eyes closed can also help them to 'see' the shape of the letter in their head.

- Introducing sets of letters which build up phonological awareness.

- Writing captions for display work.

Engaging the able child in discussion about the above activities allows the child to make connections between the marks and meanings. Adults can also model writing for the child when writing captions.

4. It is important to remember that writing for meaning does not only happen when we use a pencil and paper. Children should be encouraged to experiment with ICT to produce labels, captions and stories. More able children can use programs such as Clicker Four to 'write' their own story. Those with a good grasp of letters can begin to investigate the keyboard. The idea of the permanency of writing can be explored. They can save their work and return to it, amend it or add to it as necessary.

5. As the child's fine motor skills develop, more intricate patterns can be introduced. Curls, twists and loops all create an added challenge for the child.

Children can also be encouraged to use whiteboards and dry pens to develop gross motor and writing skills.

6. Picture closure can be introduced. Children have to follow or trace the lines of a shape or object but have the added challenge of completing the picture where the lines are missing.

4. Reading

Resources: Books – fiction and non-fiction, leaflets, environmental print, e.g. notices, labels, computer

Activity/resources	Advanced responses	Challenging activities
In the library corner	• can be regularly found in the library corner • selects a book and gives reasons for doing so, e.g. 'I like the cover; I've read about this character before.' • selects a book and studies it in detail • listens and engages in the activity	1 access to a range of books in varying styles and genres 2 access to poetry books 3 access to non-fiction books 4 book reviews
Retelling a story using a book	• can retell the story accurately • can retell the story using phrases from the book • turns pages at appropriate point • can read 'between the lines'	5 offer opportunities for the children to engage in story telling to the group 6 ask children to make up alternative endings to the story 7 build a picture from the text 8 draw a character using information from the text
Handling a book	• knows how to hold a book • knows about technical details, e.g. cover, title, author, etc. • knows where the story starts • knows how to turn pages • can follow text from right to left • looks after books	9 examine different kinds of literature 10 explore literature in a different language
Environmental print	• asks what notices round the room say • attempts to 'read' the notices using clues to predict text • keen that notices round the room should be obeyed, e.g. 'only 4 at the sand'	11 have the children help make the signs for the early years setting 12 have the children make up their own signs and notices – link to topic work 13 walk round the catchment area looking for environmental print 14 discuss new words 15 collect new words

1. Ensure that there is a range of books that lead the children into reading 'chapter books'. Some books to look out for include:

    - 'Go Bananas' series by Egmont Children's Books.

    - 'Red Fox Mini Treasures'. They include titles by Quentin Blake and Mairi Hedderwick, author of the Katie Morag books.

    - Roald Dahl's books, such as *The Enormous Crocodile* and *The Magic Finger*.

    These are tried-and-tested stories that all children find irresistible.

2. Young children often love poetry. They love the rhyming words, the rhythm of poetry and they often particularly like nonsense poetry. Ensure that poetry books are a part of the library corner. These can be read by the children themselves or as part of 'story time'.

3. Ask the children to identify areas of particular interest and offer books on these areas. Usborne and Dorling Kindersley titles are particularly useful here. Children should be encouraged to bring books from home or the library if they have a particular interest.

4. Tell the children you are thinking about adding a particular book to the library. Ask the children to review the book for you and decide if it should be included or not. This not only develops their reading skills but their reporting and reasoning skills too and it will increase their self-confidence as they realise their views are being sought and listened to.

5. Ask children to retell a story to a group of their peers. They can do this using the book or by retelling the story in their own words. They could also pre-record the story and let children listen to it. Story-telling in front of their peers allows children to develop a sense of audience and offers opportunities to develop expression, volume and voice projection.

6. Children can be asked to retell a well-known story but they have to provide an alternative ending. For example, tell the story of Jack and the Beanstalk but imagine the giant had been a kind, friendly giant instead of an angry, bad-tempered giant.

7. Encourage the children to see the 'picture' the author was trying to create. Ask them to tell you the words that build up this picture.

8. From reading a text, ask the children to paint, draw or create a character from the story using only the clues in the story to help them create the picture.

9. Have the children collect different kinds of literature, e.g. leaflets from the supermarket, museums, magazines, comics. Once they have a good collection of literature they can be encouraged to examine each kind of book, booklet, etc., and be asked to compare these with the books they have been reading and look for a comparison between:

- the style

- the layout

- the pictures

- the amount of writing

- the thickness

- the number of pages.

10. Literature from different cultures can be examined. For example, Arabic script can be discussed and the differences in how we read it explored – we read from right to left in Arabic. If you have staff or families who are Arabic speakers in your early years setting, they can be invited to talk to the children about their language and reading materials.

11. We know that involving children in rule-making means they are more likely to adhere to the rules. Having young children help to make up rules and accompanying signs can be a good way for educators to engage the children in discussion and helps to foster a sense of belonging. Children will also be able to decide what signage is required so that visitors can find their way around the early years setting. They can choose how best to produce the signs, e.g. on computer, handwritten and laminated, child's drawing, etc. Children can interview visitors to find out what signage is required. Discussions can also take place as to the height at which signs should be dis-played – signs for children will have to be placed at a lower height than signs for adults. Older children or adults can be invited in to 'follow the signs'. Can they identify key areas of the early years establishment? For example:

- the play area

- the toilets

- the office

- equipment cupboard

- the gym hall

- the music room

- the staffroom

- the headteacher's office.

12. Children can be encouraged to make up their own signs for topic work they are doing. The children could research 'real-life' signs for the topic area and then invent their own. For example, they could investigate road signs if they were studying 'my street'.

13. Children can go on an excursion outside of the early years setting to explore what kind of environmental print is around them. This can be done over a period of time and different groups can be taken to different areas so that a bank of signs is built up. Digital photographs can be taken on these excursions and a log can be built up showing key signs and aspects environmental print in the local area. Visits could be made to:

- the park

- the supermarket

- the town centre

- the village hall

- road signs

- the hospital

- the vet's

- religious buildings.

14. Discuss how children learn 'new words'. Find out how they remember new words – do they look and remember, sound the word out, remember the shape of the word if the word cannot be sounded out?

15. Children can collect 'new words' and build up a word bank. These words can be classified under headings, e.g. words from the living room:

- chair

- television

- rug

- carpet

- settee

- curtains.

Alternatively, you could use subject areas to categorise words, e.g. words we use in music:

- rhythm

- beat

- tune

- melody

- notes

- instruments.

An extra activity

Puppets are a wonderful resource to develop language skills. Early years settings should have a range of puppets on hand for children to play and engage with. Children can also make their own puppets from socks, scrap material, paper bags, etc.

Puppets can be used to:

- explore feelings – their own and the puppets'
- talk through difficult situations
- develop dialogues and conversations
- discover alternative strategies for behaviour, turn-taking, etc.

Many of these activities are adult-led. For an even richer learning experience ask the children to help you devise these.

 SUMMING UP

Some key points and suggestions have been made in this chapter in relation to challenging activities in the area of language. They include:

- the importance of developing and challenging the skills young children display in language
- a planning framework for activities
- some activities to challenge young children in their learning.

Chapter 7

Mathematics

This chapter will:

- consider why it is important to develop and challenge the skills young children display in mathematics.
- suggest a planning framework for activities
- offer some activities to challenge young children in their learning.

Early years educators need to engender a love for mathematics among the young children in their care. To do this they need to create an atmosphere conducive to mathematical thinking. They can do this by:

- celebrating mathematical thinking that takes place in the setting
- displaying mathematical work that has been done in the setting
- talking with the children about mathematical concepts
- having high mathematical expectations of the children they are working with
- encouraging children to experiment with mathematical thinking
- valuing all aspects of mathematics, not just numerical competency
- allowing children to think about mathematics so they are not always using concrete materials.

The UK appears to be facing some difficulties with regards to mathematics. International comparisons suggest that our children are doing much worse than children in other countries. There are of course inherent difficulties with such comparisons – we are not comparing like with like to start with, and scant regard is paid to significant differences, for example, children in Europe and beyond often start formal schooling much later than in the UK. Nonetheless, low achievement in the area of mathematics is something that early educators should be concerned with, if for no other reason than that the creativity and interest in mathematics that young children bring to the early years setting has to be the starting point for turning around the 'I hate maths' mindset so often prevalent in our education establishments and in society at large.

- Develop existing skills.
- Help children to transfer skills they already possess from one situation to another.
- Offer new mathematical opportunities.
- Help children of all abilities to work together.
- Help children to enjoy mathematics.

So where do we start?

One of the first things to do, regardless of what skill you are wanting to challenge, is to plan the activity. Planning an activity allows you to think about where the children are in their learning and how you would like to move their learning forward. It also offers you an opportunity to talk with the children and find out what they're interested in and how they like to learn. For example, some children will be:

- *active* learners – they like to learn by doing.
- *visual* learners – they like to learn by watching.
- *participative* learners – they like to learn by copying a more knowledgeable other.

Knowing about how the child likes to learn will help you to plan more appropriate learning tasks. Planning requires the following to be considered:

- What can the child already do?
- Is the child working independently on the skill?
- Are the present activities too easy for the child?
- What is the child interested in?
- Where do I want to take their learning next?
- What is the best way to help them get there?
- Implications for organisation.

A planning framework sheet where you can jot down some answers to these questions will allow you to think about how you will challenge a child's learning.

You can also add these to the child's folio. Over time this will result in a developmental picture of the planning that has taken place for that child.

Planning framework

With the points for good practice and the planning framework in mind, the rest of this chapter suggests activities that will allow you to challenge young children and take forward their learning.

They have been developed with the busy educator in mind. They offer ready-to-use activities that can be adapted to suit the needs of individual early years settings.

Photocopy these pages and keep them in a ring binder. You can add to them as you develop activities yourself. If you keep them in a central place, everyone can access them. This will allow your early years setting to build up a bank of challenging activities.

Question	Comment
What can the child already do?	
Is the child working independently?	
In what ways are the present activities too easy for the child?	
What do I want the child to learn? Relate to Learning Outcomes/Desirable Outcomes	
What is the best way to help them to learn?	
Implications for organisation	

CHALLENGING ACTIVITIES

1. Number

Resources: Cubes, beads, bricks, pictures, big books, the cafe, the shop

Activity/resources	Advanced responses	Challenging activities
Recognising numerals, e.g. in pictures, imaginative play, etc.	● recognises a range of numbers in various contexts ● uses number names beyond 10 ● responds to the mathematical thinking of others	1 oral work
Counting, e.g. number of currants on buns	● counts accurately ● counts reliably up to 10 and beyond	2 developing the language of number 3 counting on and counting back 4 developing number beyond 10 5 estimating
Talking about adding on, taking away	● understands the concept of adding and subtracting ● understands the concept of addition/ subtraction in the abstract ● can apply the concept within everyday situations, e.g. how many more cups do we need for snack time if there are 9 people in our group? ● recognises the symbols for adding and subtracting	6 mental maths

1. Oral work should be an integral part of mathematical work in the early years setting. Opportunities should be provided for counting items. Number cards can be used to label items so that children are secure in matching a number to the name and can do this both orally and symbolically.

2. It is important that children understand and can use the language of number. Again, oral work will be useful here as the adult establishes and challenges the language of number – one more than, one less than, higher than, lower than, greater than, smaller than. Mathematical games can be useful here: not just the playing of games but also the creating of games. For example, children can use the idea of 'snakes and ladders' to make up their own game. This involves not just mathematics but also artwork, discussion, the establishing of rules and interaction between the inventor of the game and their peers as they play with the finished product.

3. Children should be offered opportunities to count on and count back from any number. Any kind of numerical representations that are commonly found in the early years setting can help here such as:

- a number line

- a clock

- number ladders.

Children should also be introduced to numbers in both vertical and horizontal positions.

It is also useful to think about how we lay out concrete items for counting. For example, when counting on you could:

- Lay out three lion's heads in a triangular shape.

- Add another two lion's heads.

- How many heads altogether?

The layout will encourage children to count on: 3... 4, 5. Children should be encouraged to think about the various ways we can arrange items so that we can count on.

4. Able children will often be able to count well beyond 10. Where there is secure recognition of number names and digits, we can begin to develop the concept of tens and units. Children can be asked to collect and group objects into groups of 10. These should be placed in the left hoop. The remaining objects should be placed in the right hoop.

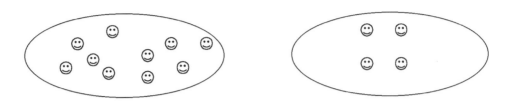

5. An important part of this work is encouraging children to 'estimate'. This can be done by:

    ● Presenting children with shapes such as:

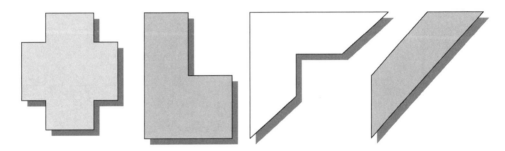

    ● Ask the children to guess how many squared coloured tiles it will take to cover the shape.

    ● Ask the children to cover and count the shapes to see how close their estimation is.

    This work also relates to area.

6. While the ability to do computation is often seen as an indicator of mathematical ability, it is argued that often young gifted mathematicians are far more interested in, patterns, for example. We should therefore be wary of asking children to start the more formal aspects of addition and subtraction as a way of challenging them. Instead we should offer them:

    ● Opportunities for engaging in 'real-life' mental mathematics. For example, when calculating something for the early years setting – we have 23 children, 4 are staying for lunch; how many are going home?

    ● Activities that involve adding on or taking away certain items. For example, I have 4 rings and 10 people. I want 3 people to stand in each ring. Do I have enough people? If not, how many more people do I need?

- Opportunities to link adding on and taking away to other mathematical concepts such as money.

- Opportunities to explore the language of number through talking about, for example, 'half of...', 'double...', 'equal share of...'.

2. Shape, position, movement and patterns

Resources: Jigsaws, puzzles

Activity/resources	Advanced responses	Challenging activities
Jigsaws, puzzles	• manipulates jigsaw pieces • can connect shape/colour of piece to shape/colour of space • knows what the final picture will be like • approaches the task logically, e.g. completes the corners first • connects the pieces with speed and ease	1 creating puzzles
Identifying shapes	• can name 2D and 3D shapes accurately • makes reference to properties of 2D and 3D shapes	2 further work on properties
Patterns and sequences	• continues patterns • orally describes pattern • copies pattern accurately	3 life patterns

1. One obvious way to challenge children in this area is to give them more complex puzzles and jigsaws, e.g. greater number of pieces, physically smaller pieces, no picture to copy, etc. Each of these is a useful and challenging activity. Another way to challenge the children is to have them make a jigsaw or puzzle themselves. This can be done in several ways:

    - give the children a blank piece of paper and ask them to cut it into different shapes and then piece it together again

    - give the children a blank piece of paper and ask them to cut it into a particular number of different shapes and then piece it together again

    - give the children a blank piece of paper and ask them to cut it into a particular number of pieces and in particular shapes; e.g. 12 pieces – four squares, four triangles and four rectangles, and then piece it together again

    - the above can be repeated but first the children can draw a picture on the paper before cutting it.

2. The use of Floor Turtles and Roamers can offer children opportunities to explore and experiment with shape, position and movement. Children can link this work to topic work being done in the early years setting. For example, if you are doing work on the hospital, children can:

- make the Floor Turtle or Roamer into an ambulance

- build a hospital from junk material

- create an 'incident' which results in people needing to be taken to hospital

- programme the Floor Turtle or Roamer to take the quickest route from the 'incident' to the hospital.

If you are working on 'myself' and the children live close to the early years setting, the children could:

- get the Floor Turtle or Roamer ready to go to the early years setting

- build a model of the early years setting

- build a model of the children's houses

- plan routes from the house to the early years setting

- features such as the swing park, the shops, granny's house can be added and will allow for a variety of routes to be developed and explored.

3. Children can:

- specify properties of shapes such as edges, corners, faces

- play with the shapes to see which roll, slide

- explore the faces of the shapes; for example, all the faces of a cube are the same; there are two triangles and three rectangles in a triangular prism

- look for 2D and 3D shapes in the world

- experiment through junk modelling

- make tiling patterns.

4. Often children in the early years are asked to 'copy patterns'. This usually involves coloured beads and cubes. Given that mathematicians argue that mathematics is all about patterns and sequences, the early years educator must widen his/her definition to include the kind of activities that foster a love of patterns and sequences. We need to allow children to explore life patterns such as:

- the seasons

- daily patterns

- weekly patterns

- yearly patterns.

Other patterns occur and should be considered, such as:

● musical patterns

● patterns in nature

● patterns in fabrics such as knitting, tweed, etc.

These kinds of patterns are often of much more interest to young able children and allow them to start to connect patterns with life around them. They will begin to see patterns everywhere and be keen to identify them and tell you about them.

● 3. Information handling

Resources: Matrices, tree diagrams, the cafe

Activity/resources	Advanced responses	Challenging activities
Sorting	● looks for imaginative ways of completing the task ● offers more than one solution ● offers more than one criterion for selection	1 sorting and connecting
Matrices and tree diagrams	● can sort on a matrix using two or more criteria ● able to identify own criteria for sorting ● will record orders accurately in the cafe using own notation or making use of prepared charts or grids	2 interpreting data

1. As with patterns and sequences, sorting is often taken to mean 'sorting items', such as modes of transport into categories. Sorting has to be viewed within the broader mathematical framework if it is to be useful. Therefore sorting is closely related to sequences, patterns and relationships. Encouraging the able child to explore, examine and explain these relationships through sorting real-life examples will be beneficial to the child and the development of their mathematical thinking. Therefore the adult must encourage children to:

● identify characteristics of living things

● identify characteristics of items

● identify characteristics in the natural world

● examine the similarities between the identified characteristics

● examine the differences between the identified characteristics

● examine the changes that occur between the identified characteristics.

2. Interpreting information is an important aspect of mathematical thinking. Able children may interpret results differently as they are thinking differently about a situation. They can connect already known facts to the new information in order to come to a new understanding. They can also 'invent' symbols to represent meaning. For example they may invent a symbol for prices in the cafe. When the meaning of this symbol is explained to all, it becomes the accepted symbol for prices in the cafe.

Building up simple graphs from information collected by the children offers opportunities for the adult to explore how children are interpreting data. It also offers opportunities to gauge how and if they are connecting this to other mathematical concepts. You could:

- find out what each child has for breakfast

- make a block graph to represent this (vertical or horizontal)

- have numerals marked on the graph but do not include details of the foods

- ask children questions about the graph.

Supply the following information about the graph:

1. The same number of people eat Shreddies as Coco Pops.

2. Only one person eats Weetabix.

3. There are twice as many people who eat Cornflakes as Rice Krispies.

4. There are two less people who eat Sugar Puffs than toast.

When working with a child at first you may not be able to start with such complicated questions. However, mathematically able children will enjoy the challenge and will soon relish the opportunity to solve the puzzle and to make up their own questions.

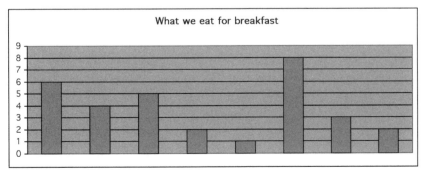

4. Money and measure

Resources: The cafe, the shop, coins, songs, rhymes, rods, rulers, height charts

Activity/resources	Advanced responses	Challenging activities
Handling money in the shop/cafe/travel agents	• understands coins have different value • can identify different coins	1 equivalent values 2 currency
Non-standard units of measurement	• measures accurately • has grasped the importance of measuring accurately • is willing to estimate • estimates are reasonably accurate • has an understanding of the comparative nature of measure • uses the language of measure appropriately	3 real-life measuring experiences

1. Adults must not forget that different children may well have a different understanding of money depending on their life circumstances. 'Saving up your pennies' will have a different meaning for a family for whom 'every penny counts' than for a child who is saving up for their second holiday abroad this year. However, equivalent values of coins will challenge the able child. Adults can ask:

   - How many different ways can you find of making 10p?

   - How many 1p make up 5p?

   - How many 50p make £1?

2. Exploring other currencies will allow the able child to:

   - know the names of different coins

   - relate coins to countries

   - compare the images on the coins

   - compare the shape of coins

   - compare the thickness of coins.

   This work links particularly well with the travel agents activity. Children's experiences of travelling abroad for family visits or holidays will also bring this to life and will reaffirm the importance of culture for the young child.

3. Measurement may involve:

   - volume

   - length

- height

- width

- capacity

- time

- mass.

It is believed that children's understanding of each of these will develop at different rates, but each is closely linked to real-life experiences.

Children can:

- engage in comparative measures; for example they can measure the table with cubes and with hand spans and then compare

- play games involving distance, such as Hopscotch

- find out how and why people measure: do all containers hold the same amount of bricks?

- investigate the capacity of various containers in the sand and water

- use a timer when playing on the computer.

AN EXTRA ACTIVITY

Early years settings could begin to see mathematical concepts in much of their everyday work. Once adults adopt this broad and real-life approach to mathematics, they can more easily include activities that foster mathematical thinking. For example:

- making a bus that will hold 10 children

- growing seeds and seeing whose grows most

- buying cakes for the early years fair

- organising the jigsaws so they all fit on the shelf

- speculating why the short, fat jug holds more milk than the tall, thin jug

- working out how many minutes it is until lunch

- leaving out construction toys, squared paper, mazes, compare bears, logiboards and pegboards and discussing mathematical concepts as a result of how the children engage with the resources.

Many of these activities are adult-led. For an even richer learning experience ask the children to help you devise these.

SUMMING UP

Some key points and suggestions have been made in this chapter in relation to challenging activities in the area of mathematics. They include:

- the importance of developing and challenging the skills young children display in mathematics

- a planning framework for activities

- some activities to challenge young children in their learning.

Chapter 8

Learning is fun and for all

In this chapter you will:

- consider why we owe it to our children to ensure they encounter challenging activities in the early years.

- think about children who have 'double exceptionality'.

- identify points for good practice.

THREADS OF LEARNING

If we look across the chapters in this book we can begin to see fine threads weaving their way through the content. These combined threads of attitude, belief, observation, identification and challenging activities allow us to make connections and to link together learning experiences. These learning experiences when considered as a whole will inform our decisions about learning:

- Is it something that excites me?

- Is it something I want to do more of?

- Is it something that I have control over?

- Is it something that I can contribute to?

Young children will be asking these questions as they engage in activities. Adults will also ponder these questions as they seek to develop practice. The developing of practice means that as adults we can influence how young children ultimately answer questions about learning. That's an exciting thought.

We know that young children want to learn. They are creative, receptive and motivated. The key is for educators to keep these sparks alive. This can be increasingly difficult in a culture that demands a more formal approach to learning earlier rather than later.

However, a failure to challenge gifted children may result in:

- underachievement

- challenging behaviour: acting-out behaviour or quiet, withdrawn behaviour

- boredom

- frustration

- an extinguishing of their natural love of learning

- a stifling of their creativity

- feelings of embarrassment in relation to their abilities

- an inability to relate to peers.

I have never met an early years educator who would want any of the above to be the end result for a child in their care. Therefore offering challenge to these children becomes a 'must' rather than an 'add-on extra'.

THE IMPORTANCE OF THE ADULT

Of key importance in the education of children are the adults in the early years setting. Adults have to:

- believe there are gifted and talented children in their early years setting

- be on the lookout for children who display particular abilities

- challenge children in their learning

- be ready to be surprised.

Early years educators need to be alert to the possibility that young gifted and talented learners may also have other labels attached to them. This is what Diane Montgomery (2003) calls 'double exceptionality'. In other words, a child may have been identified as having, for example, attention deficit hyperactivity disorder (ADHD), but given the right opportunities the same child may be equally deserving of the label 'gifted and talented'. Some common 'double exceptionalities' include:

- autistic and gifted and talented

- Asperger and gifted and talented

- social, emotional and behavioural difficulties and gifted and talented

- ADHD and gifted and talented

- dyslexic and gifted and talented

- dyspraxic and gifted and talented

- English as additional language and gifted and talented.

One of the challenges for the educator is to see past that initial label and realise that behind it lies a child with unique abilities. Offering challenging learning opportunities will allow these children to emerge from behind that first label and with help and support show what they can achieve.

DEVELOPING CITIZENS FOR THE 21ST CENTURY

It is not enough to simply challenge the academic abilities a child displays. At the same time we have to acknowledge and take account of the important part emotions and feelings play in learning. If we are serious about developing citizens for the 21st century then we have to support children holistically as they grow and develop. In other words, we have to develop the whole child. Work in this area links well to the current focus on citizenship.

Working with children in a way that acknowledges:

- their range of abilities

- their interests

- their right to be involved in the planning of their learning

- their need to work collaboratively with others

- their need to think about how they learn

- their feelings

will not only challenge them academically but will challenge them emotionally as well. As a survivor of the holocaust said:

> *Dear teacher*
>
> *I am a survivor of a concentration camp. My eyes saw what no man should witness: gas chambers built by learned engineers; children poisoned by educated physicians; infants killed by trained nurses; women and babies shot by high-school and college graduates.*
>
> *So I am suspicious of education.*
>
> *My request is: help your students to become more human. Your efforts must never produce learned monsters, skilled psychopaths, educated Eichmanns.*
>
> *Reading, writing and arithmetic are important only if they serve to make our children more human.*
>
> (Oxfam, 2002, p. 17)

We must start this process in our early years settings.

Generic points for good practice for our work with gifted and talented children in the early years setting emerge from the previous chapters. While this is not an exhaustive list, it is a good starting point for the early years setting that is seeking to develop and enhance the abilities of gifted and talented children.

- Think about what intelligence means to you.

- Look at the child holistically, gather information from a variety of sources.

- Pull that information together and use it to inform planning.

- Observe children during activities.

- Plan to challenge the child who demonstrates advanced responses.

- Offer challenging opportunities that take account of what the child can already do. This should extend to every curricular area.

- Involve the child in their learning.

- Develop the whole child.

- Never put a 'glass ceiling' on a child and their abilities; help them to reach for the stars.

These points for good practice appear in a photocopiable sheet. This will allow your early years setting to identify areas of good practice and areas for development.

Working with young learners is a privilege and, in my experience, a source of constant amazement. They consistently surprise you with their:

- insight

- humour

- sense of wonder

- love of learning

- ability to absorb knowledge

- love of life.

How are we doing?

Area for consideration?	Work still to commence	Work in progress	Work well established	Comments
An agreed definition of intelligence				
Gathering information from a variety of sources				
Use of variety of information to inform planning				
Observation of children to identify advanced responses				
Design challenging actitivities for children displaying advanced responses				
Offer challenging activities for children displaying advanced responses				
Involving the child in their learning				
Developing the whole child				
No setting of artificial limits				

Harnessing these dispositions and channelling them towards challenging learning experiences will allow children to grow and develop.

For some children, their families will offer exciting activities and be keen to develop their learning. For others, the chore of living will be enough to cope with and any formal learning that takes place may almost appear incidental. It is therefore crucial that early years settings offer a wide range of opportunities to the children in their care. Geniuses may not start as child prodigies. Similarly, exceptionally able adults were often not recognised in the early years. Practice, encouragement from significant others and development over time all played their part in creating the person they came to be. Childhood is precious. Caring for and nurturing the children in our early years settings will offer them opportunities for development – academically and emotionally.

Not all children will be given the label 'gifted and talented'. But all children do deserve to receive high-quality learning experiences that allow them to grow and develop in ways that they, and sometimes you, never thought possible.

SUMMING UP

Some key points and suggestions have been made in this chapter. They include:

- considering why we owe it to our children to ensure they encounter challenging activities in the early years

- thinking about children who have 'double exceptionality'

- identifying points for good practice.

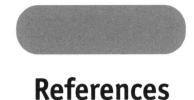

References

Bruner, J. (1996) *The Culture of Education*. Cambridge, MA: Harvard University Press.

Carr, M. (2001) *Assessment in Early Childhood Settings*. London: Sage.

Collins (1988) *The Collins Concise English Dictionary*. London: Collins.

Department for Education and Skills (1998) *Excellence for All Children: Meeting special educational needs* (Green Paper). London: DfES.

Department for Education and Skills (2001) *Special Educational Needs*. London: DfES.

Dweck. C. (1999) *Self Theories: Their role in motivation, personality and development*. Philadelphia, PA: Psychology Press.

Gardner, H. (1983) *Frames of Mind*. London: Paladin.

George, D. (1997) *The Challenge of the Able Child* (2nd edn). London: David Fulton.

Gross, M.U.M. (1993) *Exceptionally Gifted Children*. London: Routledge.

Koshy, V. and Casey, R. (1997) *Effective Provision for Able and Exceptionally Able Children*. London: Hodder and Stoughton.

McLean, A. (2003) *The Motivated School*. London: Paul Chapman.

Mares, L. (1991) *Young Gifted Children*. Melbourne: Hawker Brownlow.

Montgomery, D. (2003) *Gifted and Talented Children with Special Educational Needs*. London: Fulton.

Oxfam (2002) *Global Citizenship: The handbook for primary teaching*. Oxford: Oxfam.

Scottish Executive Education Department (2003) *Moving Forward! Additional support for learning*. Edinburgh: HMSO.

Scottish Network for Able Pupils. *Principles*. **www.ablepupils.com** (accessed 19 January 2005).

Scottish Office Education and Industry Department (1994) *Effective Provision for Special Educational Needs*. Edinburgh: HMSO.

Thurtle, V. (1997) Growth and development. In J. Taylor and M. Woods (eds) *Early Childhood Studies*. London: Arnold.

United Nations (1989) *Convention on the Rights of the Child*. UN General Assembly Document A/RES/44/25. New York: United Nations.

United Nations (1994) *Framework for Action*. Paris: UNESCO.

Glossary

Active learners – children who like to learn by doing

Alternative model of assessment – understanding is arrived at by collaboration between the adult and the learner

Contextualised learning – learning within a real-life situation or context

Double exceptionality – a child who has more than one label, e.g. 'dyslexia' and 'gifted and talented'

Entity theory of intelligence – believing a person possesses a specific amount of intelligence and nothing you or they can do will change that amount

Folk model of assessment – a set of beliefs about assessment that have grown and developed over the years

Goal achievement – performance goals are important; you have to show how clever you are

Holistic picture – gathering data from a variety of sources that allows the educator to build up a complete picture of the child and their learning

Hot-housing – pushing children on quickly through the stages of the formal curriculum

Inclusive education – children learning together: learning from each other, from adults around them and from their communities and families.

Incremental theory of intelligence – believing that intelligence is not an 'entity' that resides within a person but is something that can developed through learning

Learning goals – becoming smarter is important to you and therefore learning is important

Multiple intelligences – A range of intelligences noted by Howard Gardner. They include musical, interpersonal, logical-mathematical, etc.

Participative learners – children who like to learn by copying a more knowledgeable other

Standardised test – a test given to a group of pupils to gauge performance against either a national average (*norm-referenced*) or a breadth of subject material (*criterion-referenced*)

Tall poppies – children who are demonstrating abilities beyond what might be expected for their age

Visual learners – children who like to learn by watching

Index